BRUCE LEE

SIFU, FRIEND AND BIG BROTHER

"This book brought back a lot of fond memories of the summer days in Hong Kong in 1963 when my late brother Bruce brought back a friend of his from Seattle who stood over me like a giant but was so gentle, kind and humorous. We clicked and became close friends instantly. I am sure this beautifully written work will breathe fresh air into the life of a great legend!"

—ROBERT LEE

"It is truly a pleasure to hear Doug's personal stories about my father. I think that is where this book shines the most—in the firsthand experiences that he and he alone possess. I am grateful to Doug for sharing his memories with us all and giving us more personal insight into Bruce Lee."

—SHANNON LEE

"Doug Palmer's *Bruce Lee: Sifu, Friend and Big Brother* is a vivid, tender, and humorous recollection of a young legend in the making. Palmer's friendship with Bruce Lee boasts a privileged view into not only a masterful fighter, but a loyal son and prankster brother. Both memoir and martial arts travelogue, Palmer has the unique distinction of accompanying Lee through two rough-and-tumble, but rapidly developing cities that Lee called home. From Seattle's startling ethnic diversity in the 1960s to colonial Hong Kong's close encounters with show business and violence, Palmer takes us on a thrilling ride to understanding the heady cultures, both Eastern and Western, that inspired the Little Dragon to ascend to the highest echelon of combat arts."

—BAO TRAN, DIRECTOR, *THE PAPER TIGERS*

"With both careful detail and a friend's honesty, Doug Palmer's *Bruce Lee: Sifu, Friend and Big Brother* is a unique and rare glimpse not only into Bruce Lee's early life in America but his family life in Hong Kong as he was coming of age. There are very few people in the world that have this personal insight into the life of a legend like Palmer does, which makes this book so special to any Bruce Lee fan."

—BAO NGUYEN, DIRECTOR OF *BE WATER*

"At the age of sixteen, Doug Palmer befriended a young immigrant named Bruce Lee. The two formed a deep and lasting bond. His excellent memoir is a sympathetic tribute to a man whom he came to call Sifu, friend, and big brother, a fine study of the life of an icon who changed the world, and most of all, a poignant story wonderfully told."

— JEFF CHANG, AUTHOR, *CAN'T STOP WON'T STOP: A HISTORY OF THE HIP-HOP GENERATION*

"Growing up in Hong Kong, Bruce Lee was an undisciplined student and a punk who got into a lot of street fights. As a martial artist, he was just above average. Then he moved to Seattle in 1959 and, over the course of five years, he transformed himself and martial arts completely. Yet this crucial period remains relatively unknown. Doug Palmer's *Bruce Lee: Sifu, Friend and Big Brother* gives us a close, personal account of Bruce as a loyal friend and inspiring teacher who was constantly evolving. He makes Bruce Lee come alive against the backdrop of the early '60s, an age of innocence and transformation. A portrait of the martial artist as a young man, Doug's book is enlightening reading."

—ANG LEE, DIRECTOR, *BROKEBACK MOUNTAIN* AND *CROUCHING TIGER, HIDDEN DRAGON*

"A captivating tale about a lifelong friendship between an American from Seattle and Bruce Lee. Intelligent, well-written and engrossing from start to finish. Filled with fascinating anecdotes about the martial arts, life in Hong Kong, the movie business, and Muhammed Ali…Well worth the time."

"An insider's account of an unusual cross-cultural friendship, formed before Bruce Lee's fame took hold. Palmer didn't just study with Lee—he spent a memorable college summer in Hong Kong living with his family in 1963. He bears intimate witness to Lee's journey from outsider to international star, enriching his account with personal memories and his own considerable expertise in the martial arts."

Library of Congress Control Number: 2020940639

ISBN: 978-1-63405-985-5

Cover photo courtesy of David Tadman
Cover and book design by Dan D Shafer with Katie Meadows

CHIN MUSIC
P   R   E   S   S

Published by Chin Music Press
1501 Pike Place #329
Seattle, WA 98101-1542

First [1] edition
Paperback original

BRUCE LEE

SIFU, FRIEND AND BIG BROTHER

DOUG PALMER

Author and Bruce Lee, Hong Kong, summer 1963

TABLE OF CONTENTS

Bon Odori outside the Seattle Buddhist Temple, circa 1960s
Courtesy of the Seattle Buddhist Temple Archives

First Impressions

OWARD THE END of the evening at a Seattle street fair during the summer of 1961, I felt a tap on my shoulder. I stopped and turned around. A young Asian man stood there, a pace or two away. The circulating crowd parted and flowed around us.

He leaned slightly back from the waist, his eyes hooded, a neutral expression on his face. "I heard you were looking for me," he said.

I realized it was Bruce Lee. I had wanted to meet him after seeing him give a demonstration the week before, and had asked around to see if I could wangle an introduction. But I had heard nothing further until that evening.

The street fair, *Bon Odori*, sponsored by Seattle's Japanese-American community, was one of a number of ethnic neighborhood events every summer leading up to Seafair, a weekend of hydroplane races and air shows. In those days, the races were sometimes overshadowed by the general bacchanalian atmosphere, where participants lugged coolers of beer to the shores of Lake Washington to watch.

Bon Odori featured Japanese folk dances on a blocked-off street in front of what was then the main Buddhist "church." A milling crowd surrounded the dancers, watching or listening to the music blaring from loudspeakers, sampling *kōri* (flavored shave ice) or fried noodles from booths set up on the fringes, or just checking out the action. A friend had asked me earlier in the evening if I was still interested in meeting Bruce. I told her that I was, then forgot about it as I enjoyed the atmosphere and chatted with other kids I knew.

Facing Bruce, I was initially nonplussed. On a subconscious level, I understood that his stance, although un-menacing and not overtly martial in appearance, was one from which he was prepared to react to whatever I did. Later, I realized it was a variation of the way he taught us to stand if faced by a potentially threatening situation. The idea was to be in a position where one could defend or counter-attack instantly, yet not appear to be hostile. It gave the appearance of alertness without concern, confidence and readiness without aggressive intent. As I later found, it could indeed project the desired attitude and prevent an undesired physical confrontation.

I took Bruce's tone of voice to imply that I had been actively seeking him, perhaps for a challenge of some sort. In retrospect, I realized that in the world he came from, challenges were a part of life. Not knowing who I was or what I wanted, perhaps he thought that was a possibility.

I stuck out my hand and introduced myself. But in doing so, I purposely refrained from stepping closer to him. Rather, I leaned forward from the waist, extending my hand out for a long awkward handshake. I told him that I had seen his recent demonstration in Chinatown, and was interested in taking lessons.

He thought it over, then shrugged noncommittally and told me when they practiced. "Drop by sometime, check it out," he said. "If you're still interested, we'll see."

He melted back into the crowd. I had no idea where they practiced, or how I was going to get there. But I was ecstatic. One way or another, I would find a way to show up.

———————

AT THE TIME, I knew next to nothing about Bruce Lee. Only his name and a first impression from the demo of Chinese martial arts I had seen the week before at another street fair, in Seattle's Chinatown.

The demo was performed on a stage erected on one of the blocked-off streets by Bruce and three of his students. He called the martial art *gung fu*,[1] a name I had never heard before.

I had just finished my junior year in high school. I had boxed since fifth grade, with a bout early on as a paperweight on a TV show called Madison Square Kindergarten. When I saw Bruce's demonstration, my latest bout had been as part of a team that boxed the inmates at the state reformatory in Monroe. I had friends who practiced judo and had heard of karate—as a kid, I had even bought a bogus book on karate I'd seen advertised in the back of a comic book. But *gung fu* was a total unknown. At the time, I was unaware that it had a long history in China, or that it was then taught in Chinatowns across the U.S. only to Chinese.

When Bruce stood up there on the stage in his black *gung fu* uniform, he didn't seem all that impressive at first. He looked rather slender, smaller than a high school running back, not even a welterweight. The three students who assisted in the demonstration, one black, one white, the third Asian, were all older and more imposing physically. But once Bruce moved, he commanded the stage.

When he moved, he literally exploded. His hands were just a blur; the power in his snapping fists was palpable as he missed his students' noses by millimeters. As a boxer, I appreciated the moves he made with his hands. But the legs added a whole new dimension. The need to defend against kicks to the shin, knee or groin, or higher, signaled what seemed like a total fighting system. I was blown away.

Two other aspects of the demonstration also made an impression. One was the exotic grace of a praying mantis form he executed. It was quite unlike anything I had ever seen before. The second thing that stuck with me was the demonstration of *chi sau*, or sticking hands. Once he closed with his opponent and their wrists came in contact, he deflected all attempted blows and launched counterattacks with his eyes closed. I had never seen anything like that, either.

Much later, I found out that Bruce had given a demonstration over a year before I first saw him, at a function where I had boxed one night, but I never saw him then. The function was a Fight Night put on by a Seattle University fraternity in the university gym, just a few blocks from where Bruce was then living—a "smoker," as such nights of boxing matches were then called. I was in the first of six bouts. According to the program, a copy of which someone showed me decades after Bruce died, the first six matches were followed by an event called "**JACK MONREAN** wrestles **THE UNMASKED KNIGHT**," followed by another boxing match, and then by a "Chinese Boxing—Judo Demonstration" featuring Bruce against some *judoka* named Masafusa Kimura. After that was an intermission and the presentation of an "Ugly Man Plaque."[2]

Since at that time I was only a sophomore in high school, barely fifteen years old and not yet driving, I was compelled to rush home right after my fight. As a consequence, I missed the Chinese boxing/judo match, if that's what it was. Otherwise, I may have tried to hook up with Bruce even sooner than I did. Knowing Bruce (and his flair for showmanship), and since the program lists Ed Chow, the son of his landlord Ping and Ruby Chow, as being the commentator, I suspect the demonstration was a highly orchestrated affair highlighting the differences between the two disciplines, with Bruce showcasing his "Chinese boxing" to advantage. Since the *judoka* showed up several months later on the side of a karate man who challenged Bruce, perhaps he was offended by the experience.

In any event, it was to be more than a year after that before I was destined to run across him again, in 1961. Watching his powerful demonstration of *gung fu* at the street fair in Chinatown (now called the International District, or Seattle Chinatown/ID), I was mesmerized by the revelation of a whole new world. I vowed to myself that I would find a way to meet Bruce, and to learn from him this exotic new fighting system.

It didn't take long to figure out a line of approach. The high school I attended, Garfield, was in Seattle's Central Area. The student body was black, white and Asian, roughly a third each. I had a number of Chinese friends, and began to ask around. As it turned out, the younger brother of a classmate, Jacquie Kay, was taking lessons from Bruce. Jacquie was also a friend of Ruby Chow's daughter, and Bruce spent a lot of time at Jacquie's house, enjoying her mom's home-cooked meals, talking with her father and drawing with her younger brother. I asked her to arrange an introduction, but heard nothing further until *Bon Odori*.

BRUCE LEE WAS a revolutionary. He revolutionized the martial arts world, and the way martial arts were portrayed in film. He overturned our stereotype of the Asian male (as being subservient and asexual), and brought an appreciation of the martial arts to a mainstream audience. His approach to the martial arts, and to life, influenced many people in other disciplines as well.

He also had a major influence on my life. That time I first saw him on that stage, I was sixteen. He was only four years older than I

ALPHA PHI OMEGA'S

Second Annual

Fight Night

Masafusa Kimura
Bruce Lee.

FRIDAY

April 8, 1960

8:00 P.M.

Seattle University Gym

THE CHAMBER

"Contemporary Moods"

Stereo   Refreshments

Program

PART ONE

EXHIBITION

TOMMY SAUBER vs. DOUG PALMER

EDDIE HUBBARD vs. GILL HAYNE

TOM SELL vs. PAUL MAFFEO

FRANK LARA vs. CLARK STUMP

JERRY CARR vs. PETE QUAEMPTS

FRANK RING vs. NED FLOHR

JACK MONREAN wrestles THE UNMASKED KNIGHT

GARY WILSON vs. STAN STRICHERZ

Chinese Boxing—Judo Demonstration

BRUCE LEE vs. MASAFUSA KIMURA

ED CHOW, *Commentator*

INTERMISSION

PRESENTATION OF UGLY MAN PLAQUE

GARSKI'S SCARLET TREE

"Dining with Atmosphere" — Organ Music Nightly

66th and Roosevelt   10:00 - 2:00

Full courses   Daily was—still 20. Close enough in age to be a friend, yet older enough to be a teacher (*sifu*) and, in many ways, like an older brother. Over the next decade, including a summer spent with him and his family in Hong Kong, I learned from him not only martial arts, but also many valuable life lessons that stuck with me and served me many times in good stead.

By the time of his death his name had gained international recognition; afterwards, his influence mushroomed exponentially into a planet-wide phenomenon. He had the huge impact he did not just because he was a genius and a physical prodigy. His physical attributes are well-known, including preternatural speed and coordination, and exceptional strength for his size. Those attributes drew others to him, myself included. But he also possessed a formidable array of other qualities that were equally important: determination, self-discipline, persistence to the point of being a perfectionist, self-confidence, open-mindedness to new ideas and people, a willingness to share, a flair for showmanship, a subtle sense of humor that could be self-deprecating, a personal character that combined loyalty, a sense of dignity, and a respect for others.

Because he sometimes seemed larger than life, his subtlety and complexity could be overlooked. Some of his positive attributes at times verged on excess, the *yang* overwhelming any trace of *yin*. His self-confidence could come across as arrogance, his single-mindedness as self-absorption. But he was constantly assessing, taking stock, tinkering, not just with his martial arts but with his own character. In the end, he eliminated the strains that held him back, honing his arsenal of abilities to their maximum effect.

In his family's words, when Bruce left Hong Kong for the States at the age of eighteen he was a "good to above average" martial artist, and when he returned four years later he manifested a "very special talent that is rarely found on this earth."[3] When I first met him he was a work in progress, and he was still evolving the last time I saw him nine months before he died.

In the chapters that follow, I hope to share the Bruce I knew, to let you see the qualities that made him the person he was, that made him so special not only to the people whose lives he touched directly, but to those around the world for whom he became an inspiration.

ENDNOTES

1 I spell *gung fu* with a "g" (rather than *kung fu*, the spelling most are familiar with) because that was how Bruce usually spelled it. That spelling also more closely represents its actual pronunciation than *kung fu*, a spelling which is an artifact of a particular system for romanizing spoken Mandarin, now on the wane. In *pinyin*, the romanization system used in China, it is spelled *gongfu*. Bruce was a native Cantonese speaker, but it so happens that the term *gung fu* is pronounced more or less the same in both Cantonese and Mandarin Chinese.

2 The smoker and demo were on April 8, 1960. See the program for the event, shown in this chapter.

3 *Lee Siu Loong: Memories of the Dragon,* by Bruce's siblings and compiled by David Tadman, p. 6.

Bruce and his car, Seattle, circa 1960
Courtesy of the Bruce Lee Family Archive

CHAPTER 2
The Road to Seattle

B RUCE'S FATHER WAS a well-known Cantonese opera and movie star. Toward the end of 1939, he went on an extended tour of Chinatowns across the United States. Bruce was born during the tour, in San Francisco, on November 27, 1940. It was not only the Year of the Dragon, but also the hour of the dragon in the Chinese zodiac, the dragon often considered the most propitious of the twelve zodiac signs.

His parents named him "Jun Fan" (spelled "Jun Fon" on his birth certificate) in Cantonese, which could be interpreted as "Shaking Up San Francisco."[4] The nickname he was given as a child by his family was "Mo Si Ting," or "Never Sits Still,"[5] because of his restlessness. But the name that he came to be known as later was "Siu Lung," or "Little Dragon," his stage name as a child actor in Hong Kong.

His mother, Grace Ho, was Eurasian. The extent and origin of her European blood is a matter of some uncertainty. Her father was a prominent Chinese business man who was ostensibly half Dutch, but may have been entirely Chinese. Her mother may have been a Eurasian concubine, or a secret mistress who was entirely English.[6] Doing the math, that would mean that Bruce was anywhere from one-eighth to three-eighths Caucasian. He didn't try to hide that, but I recall him only mentioning the fact that he was part white in passing. Throughout the time I knew him he proudly identified as Chinese.

When he was born, the Second Sino-Japanese War had been waging for several years. The Japanese occupied much of northern China and various coastal areas, including areas around Hong Kong, which was then a British Crown Colony. Some of his father's opera colleagues chose to stay in the U.S., or were stranded there when war broke out between Japan and the U.S. One of those was Ping Chow, who eventually ended up in Seattle and with his wife Ruby opened a restaurant there, called "Ruby Chow's." Since Bruce's parents had left their three older children in Hong Kong with his paternal grandmother, then 70, their choice to return was not really much of a choice.

Bruce and his parents left San Francisco to return to Hong Kong when Bruce was less than six months old, arriving by boat in May of 1941. He soon became dangerously ill and nearly died. Several months later, in December, several hours after the attack on Pearl Harbor, the Japanese invaded Hong Kong. Bruce was nearly five when the Japanese surrendered and Hong Kong reverted back to being a British colony. When he started school, he was still a skinny kid. He was also near-sighted and wore thick glasses. He was often picked on, but fought back.[7]

By all accounts, the Japanese occupation of Hong Kong was brutal; the British, although less brutal, left no doubt as to who was in charge. Both periods left an imprint on his character.

He had no problem tapping into Chinese nationalist feelings in his movies. His second movie in Hong Kong after unsuccessfully trying to break into Hollywood, *Fist of Fury*, made in 1972 with Japanese martial artists as the primary villains, was set in Shanghai during the early 20th century. Sections of the city were then controlled by foreign powers. In one scene, he is denied entry to a park with a sign that declares "No Dogs or Chinese Allowed." After being taunted by a Japanese man who tells him that if he behaves like a dog, he will be allowed in, he beats up the man and his friends and kicks the sign to smithereens.

Recent scholarship has cast doubt on whether or not signs with that exact wording ever existed, but their existence was unquestioned in the Chinese public mind as a symbol of Chinese humiliation by foreign powers. Bruce certainly believed that such signs were a reality in Hong Kong before the war and during the Japanese occupation.

But as much as the Japanese occupation left its mark on him, Bruce never evidenced any prejudice or ill will toward individual Japanese. His first serious girlfriend in Seattle, Amy Sanbo, to whom he proposed, was a Japanese-American, as was his good friend and assistant, Taky Kimura, who ran the Seattle *gung fu* school when Bruce later moved to California. When I introduced him to the woman I was to marry, Noriko Goto, a student from Japan, he was gracious and welcoming. There were also other Japanese from Japan that he befriended.

He was certainly aware of the history of the Japanese occupation of Hong Kong, and undoubtedly heard stories from his parents and others, but probably had few direct memories of his own from that period. In any event, he seemed to have no problem in separating his views of individual Japanese from his views of Japan's historical occupation of China and Hong Kong.

His attitudes toward the British, on the other hand, seemed more visceral, perhaps because he encountered them as real people as he was growing up, particularly in the form of sailors on leave in Hong Kong. On more than one occasion I heard him tell of run-ins with British sailors who were over-confident in facing what seemed like a skinny bespectacled Chinese kid much smaller than they. One of Bruce's techniques, when the sailor raised his hands in a boxing stance, was to clap his hands and yell, to focus the sailor's attention on his hands, followed quickly with a straight snapping kick to the groin. He and his posse also tangled with British students from another high school.

British sailors and students were not the only ones Bruce brawled with as a teenager. The Hong Kong streets were tough, and according to Bruce as well as his family he got in fights constantly. But although he had practiced some *t'ai chi* with his father, he wasn't into it and hadn't yet had any formal *gung fu* training when he first began getting into scrapes. His first formal lessons were from Yip Man, a well-known teacher of Wing Chun. Most accounts say he started with Yip Man in 1953, when he was thirteen, but one claims that it wasn't until after getting kicked out of his first high school (Lasalle) and starting a new one (St. Francis Xavier) in September of 1956, when he was still fifteen.[8]

His main instructors at Yip Man's school were apparently two older students, William Cheung and Wong Shun Leung. The reason for that may have been that some of his fellow students tried to get him expelled from the school (using the fact that he wasn't "pure Chinese" as one of their arguments), and as a compromise Yip man had him study with Wong and avoid the main class for a while.[9] Wong was an experienced and renowned street fighter who mentored Bruce, encouraging him to hone his classroom skills both on the streets and in bare knuckle matches on rooftops against other *gung fu* schools. Bruce's fights did not slow down; if anything, they became more frequent.

By the time he was eighteen, his family had decided he needed a fresh start. In April of 1959 they literally shipped him off to the States on an ocean liner in third class with a grubstake of a hundred dollars, before he had even graduated from high school.

I have read various versions of the reason for his leaving so precipitously, including that he defeated the son of a triad leader in a fight and that he needed to leave town to avoid a contract that was out on him. In another more credible version,[10] he beat up the son of a powerful family that complained to the police, who warned his parents that he would be arrested if he didn't shape up. I never heard Bruce mention the exact reasons for him being packed off to the States, but he spoke often about his numerous fights and all accounts seem to agree that his family sent him off because he was constantly in trouble in Hong Kong. The fact that he was already an American citizen perhaps suggested the solution.

He was by then a well-known child movie actor, but that did not dissuade his parents from sending him away. In fact, his father had forbade him from acting in any movies for several years as a punishment for his misbehavior. Ironically, just as he was preparing to leave he was allowed to appear in one last film, *The Orphan*, which increased his popularity in Hong Kong as a star dramatically. But the die was already cast.

Three more matters of note occurred in the year or so prior to his departure. One was the proficiency he gained in the cha-cha, even winning a Hong Kong-wide cha-cha contest in 1958. He applied the same skill he did in mastering *gung fu* forms to choreographing his dance moves. The cha-cha was one of his few passions outside of the martial arts, and served as an ice-breaker in social situations. On the boat over to the States he gave lessons to passengers in upper-deck cabins, and he carried a card with his 108 different cha-cha moves in his wallet for many years.[11]

The second matter was his one foray into martial arts as modified for sport—an intermural boxing match he was persuaded to participate in by one of the teachers at his high school. Although Bruce won the bout handily, against an opponent who had won that weight division for the three previous years, knocking him down repeatedly, he was frustrated by the limitations of his punching power with boxing gloves and his inability to put his opponent down for the count.[12] Although in later years he used modified boxing gloves and other equipment for sparring, the experience solidified his distaste for contests with restraining rules or gear. He forswore competing in any karate-style competitions where points were awarded for landing punches or kicks in circumscribed areas, and insisted in his real matches that they be full contact with no rules of engagement as to where or how one could strike.

Lastly, in the few months before his departure he learned some showier forms and techniques from a teacher of northern style *gung fu*, including a basic praying mantis set. He was already thinking of teaching *gung fu* in the States, to augment his income. He figured he could teach the northern styles to students who wanted showmanship, and Wing Chun to those who valued practicality.[13]

When it was time to leave, his family and friends saw him off at the dock. After an ocean voyage of more than two weeks, he landed in the city of his birth.

BRUCE STAYED IN San Francisco for the summer with a friend of his father. He lasted only a week as a waiter at a restaurant where his father's friend got him a job, but made some pocket money teaching cha-cha in San Francisco Chinatown and across the Bay in Oakland.[14]

In early September of 1959, Bruce moved up to Seattle to finish high school. Fook Yeung, another old friend of his father, then a chef at a Seattle restaurant, drove down from Seattle to bring him up.[15] From then until he went back to Hong Kong to visit his family in the spring of 1963, he lived at Ruby Chow's Restaurant and worked there as a dishwasher, busboy and waiter. Fook Yeung was also a *gung fu* practitioner, mainly a devotee of the Praying Mantis school, and soon taught Bruce some of its forms.[16]

Ruby Chow's was an eponymous restaurant located in Seattle on the corner of Broadway and Jefferson, a short block or so away from the parking garage where Bruce later taught his classes. It was one of the first higher-end Chinese restaurants in Seattle outside of Chinatown, if not the first, and most of the customers were non-Chinese, including local political figures.

The restaurant building was an old Seattle wood-frame mansion that had been retro-fitted into a restaurant with boarding rooms upstairs. Bruce lived on the second floor in a room that was more like a walk-in closet, located partly underneath a stairway leading up to the third floor. I never saw his room, but by all accounts it was sparsely furnished, with the bathroom down the hall. According to Skip Ellsworth, one of Bruce's early students, Bruce slept on a mattress directly under the sloped ceiling on the underside of the stairway, with his clothes neatly folded and stacked alongside. A wooden fruit-box served as a desk; a single naked light-bulb hung down on a wire from the ceiling, above the fruit-box.[17]

Ruby was a formidable woman with a beehive hairdo and a strong personality, a powerhouse in Seattle's Chinese community who later became the first Asian-American elected to the King County Council. Ruby expected Bruce to work for his keep and put up with the high-handed behavior which some of her customers displayed. To say that Ruby and Bruce had a personality clash

Bruce in front of Ruby Chow's, Seattle, circa 1960
Courtesy of the Bruce Lee Family Archive

would be understating it. No doubt she thought of him as a young whipper-snapper, an ungrateful freeloader who expected to be treated as a pampered houseguest.

Ed Chow, Ruby Chow's eldest son, a year-and-a-half older than Bruce, was the commentator for the "Chinese boxing—judo demonstration" at the Seattle University fraternity smoker the following April given by Bruce and a Japanese *judoka*. I don't know if Ed was attending Seattle University at the time, but the campus was practically next door to the restaurant. Perhaps some students or faculty were customers at the restaurant and came across Bruce there.

Bruce was also well-known for his sense of humor and corny jokes. One of his favorite jokes perhaps resonated with him because of his experience at Ruby Chow's, straining to keep his temper in check when he was treated poorly by a boorish customer. As told by Bruce with his distinctive panache, an American walks into a Chinese restaurant, sits down and orders fried rice. The Chinese waiter replies, "OK, one fly lice." The American laughs and says, "No, Charlie, it's not 'fly lice'—it's *'fried rice.'*" After that, every time the American would come into the restaurant he would tease the waiter and yell out, "Hey Charlie, get me some 'fly lice!'" The waiter grew very annoyed at this, so he began practicing the correct pronunciation at home. Bruce would imitate the waiter practicing at home in front of a mirror, gradually improving his pronunciation until he could say "fried rice" perfectly. The waiter could barely contain himself until the next time the American walks into the restaurant and calls out, "Hey Charlie, get me some 'fly lice!'" Whereupon the waiter marches over and draws himself up proudly to confront the American. "It's not 'fly lice'—it's *'fried rice,'*" the waiter says, enunciating slowly and carefully. *"You Amelican plick!"* Bruce would deliver the last line with gusto in a stereotypical Chinese accent and then crack himself up.

In any event, Bruce spent as little time as possible at the restaurant, and I got the distinct sense that he was counting the days until he could move out on his own. But he put up with it for nearly four years, until he returned to Seattle from a visit back to Hong Kong in 1963. I sometimes wonder if he needed to get the blessing of his father to move out, since his father had arranged for him to stay with Ping and Ruby in the first place. Most likely, it took a while for him to build up the confidence that he could make it on his own, teaching *gung fu* classes. By the time he went back to Hong Kong he was earning enough money that he could make the move.

Soon after arriving in Seattle he also enrolled at Edison Technical School to get his high school diploma. The building where Edison was housed, on Broadway in the Capitol Hill neighborhood, is now part of the Seattle Central Community College campus. His first *gung fu* students were fellow students at Edison.

In addition to working at Ruby Chow's and going to school, he continued his *gung fu* training. He had a wooden dummy shipped from Hong Kong, which he would pound away at to practice his *chi sau* and strengthen his forearms.[18] He also began to participate in demonstrations, including with Fook Yeung.[19]

BRUCE WAS STREET-WISE in Hong Kong, but was still learning the way things worked in America. So it was not surprising that he was drawn to some of his fellow students at Edison, who were older and packed full of hard-earned street smarts from this side of the ocean, and who became his first students.

The first one was Jesse Glover, a husky black man with a brown belt in judo. Jesse was then twenty-six, six years older than Bruce. He first saw Bruce in a demo in which Bruce appeared with the Chinese Youth Club, following a cha-cha performance which Bruce put on. Jesse had recently returned from California, in an unsuccessful attempt to find a *gung fu* teacher, so he was excited when he learned of the upcoming *gung fu* demo in his back yard. Jesse was impressed with what he saw, and vowed he was going to learn to move the same way.[20]

Jesse has written that he started learning *gung fu* from Bruce in 1959 after seeing Bruce in a summer Seafair exhibition.[21] But Bruce didn't arrive in Seattle until September of 1959, long after the summer Seafair events were over. And his diary suggests that it wasn't until January of the following year that he first met Jesse and began teaching him. His entry for Friday, January 8, 1960[22] reads:

> To day after school, a negro came and ask me to teach him Kung
> Fu. He is a brown belt holder of judo and weighs 180 lb. However,
> I think he is kind of clumsy. If he practice under my instruction,
> I'm sure he can achieve distinction.

Two days later, on Sunday, he made another diary entry:

> To day I went to the negro's house and teach him a few tricks on
> Kung Fu and ask him not to use it on Chinese! Tonight I couldn't
> go to sleep.

Jesse quickly realized that Bruce had some unique skills and started working out with him, initially one on one in Jesse's apartment and at school and other odd locations when they could grab the time.[23] Ruby didn't like Bruce teaching non-Chinese, so they couldn't practice at the restaurant.[24]

At that time, Bruce was still developing his own style, experimenting with techniques from other *gung fu* schools. He taught Jesse different ways to attack and defend so he could practice against them. As Jesse put it, "the only reason that I learned what I did was because at the time he needed a live dummy to train on." A lot of the techniques were ones Bruce discarded, or simply filed away without passing them on when he later started teaching formal classes.[25]

Jesse also tells that when they first met, Bruce thought of his own skill level as being little more than an advanced beginner. He made trips up to Vancouver, B.C.'s Chinatown to buy books on different *gung fu* styles, then devoured them once back in Seattle; his dream was to learn the secrets of the masters of the various styles and combine them into a "super system." For a while he was a strong believer in forms, but within a year changed his mind and discounted any system that emphasized forms.[26]

Bruce also trained a few others who were introduced by Jesse. The second student was Ed Hart, also a judo man and formidable street fighter, who roomed with Jesse. Howard Hall, another Edison student, and Pat Hooks, Skip Ellsworth and Charlie Woo, all judo men, soon joined. By then, the group had outgrown Jesse's apartment.

By early February 1960 Bruce had met Taky Kimura through Jesse. Taky was a black belt in judo and Bruce spent hours working out with Taky in judo at the YMCA.[27] After a while Bruce incorporated his new students into his demonstrations, but I believe that was after the April 1960 demo at the Seattle U smoker. By September LeRoy Garcia, whose wife went to Edison and had seen one of Bruce's demos, had joined the group.

At first, it was Bruce and his fellow students exchanging martial arts techniques and working out together. According to Jim DeMile, a 225-pound, super heavyweight boxer in the Air Force who was also introduced by Jesse, Bruce was "a kid with some neat skills we wanted to learn," and when they hung out after training together "we were just a bunch of guys having a good time and Bruce was just one of those guys."[28] Bruce no doubt learned a lot

2 月 6 日

19 _60_. 曜日   天候

To-day at around 12:30 took Yeung, Jesse and I went down to the YMCA where we met Kimura (2nd dan black belt) All of them are impressed by my Gung Fu and ask me to teach them.

Bruce's diary, February 6, 1960
Courtesy of the Bruce Lee Family Archive

from them too, especially how techniques needed to be adjusted to deal with larger opponents than he was used to dealing with. Jesse also helped Bruce with adjustment problems in his new environment, including difficulty in speaking in front of others.[29] But it was clear that they greatly valued Bruce's superior skills in the martial arts. Although it was a mutual voyage of discovery, Bruce was the one driving the boat.

Although Jesse eventually went his own way, he had tremendous respect for Bruce and referred to himself throughout his life as Bruce's "first student." He also unabashedly said that Bruce was "far ahead" of him, and that he "couldn't hit Bruce if [he] had tried." He went on to say that since Bruce was his "teacher," he wouldn't have tried anyway.[30] Jim DeMile and Bruce had a falling-out early on, but he always spoke highly of Bruce's unparalleled ability as a fighter.[31]

When the number of students Bruce was training grew larger,

they started practicing in playfields and various other outdoor locations. By March of 1961 there were ten students who chipped in ten dollars each per month to rent some space in Chinatown.[32] By May, with many of the students out of work, they had to give up the space; Bruce stopped teaching temporarily and took a part-time job outside of Ruby Chow's to tide him over financially.[33] When I joined the class, the group practiced in LeRoy Garcia's back yard.

One diary entry gives an interesting insight into Bruce's personality in his early years in Seattle. In early 1960 an entry mentions a "small scrap" he had had, noting that he had "better learn more patience and practice self-defence a little more."[34]

———

WHILE HE WAS still at Edison, some months before I joined the class, Bruce was challenged by a karate man who also had a black belt in judo.[35] According to Jesse, the karate man had a reputation for picking fights with tough opponents, and winning.

It is not clear when the match took place, but I would guess it was around November of 1960. Jesse describes the fight as taking place after a demo Bruce and his students put on at Yesler Terrace gym which, from a poster in Jesse's book, was on October 28, 1960. The karate man challenged Bruce after the demo, but Bruce declined after checking with his students to make sure they would not think any less of him. The pretext for the challenge was that the karate man had taken umbrage over a comment Bruce made about soft styles being better than hard styles. Bruce was referring to *gung fu* styles, but apparently the karate man thought Bruce was talking about karate. Over the ensuing days, the fellow became more and more obnoxious at school. Eventually Bruce's patience ran out, and Jesse arranged for them to meet for a no-holds-barred, bare-knuckled match.[36]

Bruce and some of his earliest students, Seattle, circa 1960
Standing left to right: Pat Hooks, Bruce, Ed Hart, Jesse Glover
Kneeling left to right: Taky Kimura, Charlie Woo, Leroy Porter
Courtesy of the Bruce Lee Family Archive

The match took place on a YMCA handball court. Present on Bruce's side were Jesse, who acted as referee and Bruce's second, Ed Hart, who acted as the timekeeper, Howard Hall and LeRoy Garcia. On the karate man's side was Masafusa Kimura, the *judoka* who gave the demo with Bruce at the Seattle U smoker, and another student from Japan. The fight was supposed to go three two-minute rounds, with the winner being the one who won two of the three rounds. A round was won by knocking a man down or out. If someone was unable to continue, he lost. The challenger changed into his karate *gi*, complete with black belt. Bruce kept his street clothes but took off his shirt, shoes and socks.

Bruce waited for the challenger to make the first move, a snap front kick. Bruce swept it aside and attacked with a flurry of straight punches which in Jesse's words "tore his opponent apart." He finished with a kick to the face as the challenger dropped. Jesse went on to say, "When the guy hit the floor he didn't move for a long time and we thought he was dead." It turned out that Bruce had cracked his opponent's skull around his eye and down into his cheekbone.

The entire encounter lasted something like eleven seconds, but when the challenger came to and asked how long it had lasted, Ed Hart felt bad and told him it had taken twice as long.[37]

When Bruce blocked the first kick, Jesse saw that it had brushed Bruce's tank top undershirt, and thought "if the guy's leg was a little longer or the kick was a little quicker that the fight might have taken a different path." Shortly after that, according to Jesse, Bruce changed his tactics and decided it was better to carry the attack to an opponent rather than wait and counter.

Bruce did not hold grudges, however. The karate man later wanted to learn from Bruce. He wanted Bruce to give him private instructions, but Bruce told him he would have to join the class like everyone else.[38]

ENDNOTES

4   The character for "Jun," which may have been changed from a slightly different one when he was young, means to "shake, move or excite to action." The character for "Fan" literally means "boundary" or "frontier," but was also used as part of the transliteration of "San Francisco," the "Fan" being similar in sound to "Fran."

5   Linda Lee, *The Bruce Lee Story*, p. 27. (The book uses an incorrect romanization of the nickname, which Linda pointed out to me.)

6   The Lee family has described Grace's heritage at various times as being part German or part German and English, as well as Chinese. See *Bruce Lee: A Life* by Matthew Polly, note to p. 13 citing brother Robert's book, and *Bruce Lee: Words of the Dragon (2017 edition)*, edited by John Little, note 8 on p. 69. I vaguely recollect being told by the family that she was part White Russian (the term used for the people who fled Russia in the wake of the Russian Revolution). When I asked Robert a few years ago, he confirmed that she was Eurasian but said he regretted that he had never inquired about the details. Her father, Ho Kom Tong, was raised as the son of a Dutch Jew named Charles Maurice Bosman, who emigrated to Hong Kong and became a successful entrepreneur, and a Chinese concubine from Shanghai. But there is some question as to whether Bosman was really Ho Kom Tong's father. During an exit interview on the eve of his parent's return to Hong Kong, in order to document Bruce as an American citizen and preserve his ability to re-enter the United States, his mother clearly stated that her mother was English and had no Chinese blood. But there is still some question about that, too. See Charles Russo's book, *Striking Distance: Bruce Lee and the Dawn of Martial Arts in America*, p. 50. In *Bruce Lee: A Life*, Matthew Polly asserts that her father was indeed half Chinese and half Dutch-Jewish, and that her mother was 100% English. See pp. 13-14 and chapter notes thereto. But from the notes, it is clear that he is speculating. His notes also mention that the Dutch-Jewish Bosman family could be traced to Germany several generations before, which could explain the origin of the claim that Grace was part German.

7   Linda Lee, *The Bruce Lee Story*, p. 144; Polly, *A Life*, pp. 24,35.

8   See, e.g., Russo, *Striking Distance*, p. 53, and his notes thereto on p. 177, citing several sources; and in his introduction to Bruce's *Chinese Gung Fu: The Philosophical Art of Self-Defense*, James Lee, on p. 1, states that Bruce started with Yip Man at age thirteen. Linda also confirms that Bruce always said he started with Yip man when he was thirteen. The only account I've seen claiming that Bruce didn't start with Yip Man until he was fifteen is Matthew Polly, *Bruce Lee: A Life*, pp. 46 and 52-55. His argument appears to be mainly based on an article by Hawkins Cheung, a teenage pal of Bruce's, who says that he met Bruce at St. Francis Xavier after which they started with Yip Man together. Hawkins Cheung, "Bruce Lee's Hong Kong Years," *Inside Kung-Fu*, November 1991. But the introduction to the article states that Hawkins began his training with Yip Man in 1953 (i.e., when Bruce was thirteen). In any event, if Bruce did start with Yip Man when he was fifteen, rather than thirteen, the strength of the platform he built with Wing Chun is even more remarkable. (Jesse Glover, Bruce's first student, says Bruce told him he studied Wing Chun for four years, which is somewhere in between. Jesse Glover, *Bruce Lee*, p. 13.)

9   Polly, *A Life*, p. 54.

10 Ibid., pp. 71-72.

11 Linda Lee, *The Bruce Lee Story*, pp. 30, 35.

12 Polly, *A Life*, pp. 60-61.

13 Hawkins Cheung, "Bruce Lee's Hong Kong Years," *Inside Kung-Fu*, November 1991.

14 Russo, *Striking Distance*, pp. 29-30, 47-48.

15 Paul Bax, *Number One: Reflections from Bruce Lee's First Student, Jesse Glover*, p. 49. According to Bruce's daytimer, he arrived in Seattle on September 3, 1959. Fook Yeung's name is also sometimes spelled "Fook Young." Jesse described Fook Yeung as a cook at Ruby Chow's but LeRoy Garcia, another early student, remembers him as being a chef at The Polynesia, a waterfront restaurant.

16 According to a teacher of the Praying Mantis in New York, Gin Foon Mark, Bruce's father made a trip to New York City with his opera troupe shortly after Bruce arrived in San Francisco, and Bruce flew back to join him in June of 1959. Mark claimed that Bruce sparred with one of his students and they appeared about evenly matched; and that since Mark's student had only been practicing for about a year, that did not sit well with Bruce. Mark also claimed that he changed Bruce's stance so that his right arm was held further from the body, and introduced him to more fluid footwork. The source for this account is mainly *The Dragon and the Tiger*, by Greglon Yimm Lee and Sid Campbell. In an interview he gave to Paul Bax, Gin Foon Mark has told a similar story. But I have never heard of this from any other source, and I doubt this claim. For one thing, I don't think Bruce's father traveled to New York right after Bruce arrived in San Francisco. In addition, Mark claims Bruce at that time wanted him to go out to California to instruct him and be a consultant for his films, but this was long before Bruce got involved in the movie business in Hollywood. Jesse Glover, Bruce's first student, also never heard mention of such trip, and had his doubts. According to Jesse, Bruce learned his Praying Mantis forms from Fook Yeung. Jesse Glover, *Bruce Lee*, pp. 13, 16 and 65; and Paul Bax, *Number One: Reflections from Bruce Lee's First Student, Jesse Glover*, pp. 34 and 212. LeRoy Garcia also confirms that Fook Yeung taught Bruce a lot.

17 Paul Bax, ed., *Bruce Lee: Disciples of the Dragon*, digital version, interview with Skip Ellsworth, pp. 47-48.

18 In a letter to Hawkins Cheung, a childhood friend, written May 16, 1960, he mentions the wooden dummy that he had had shipped from Hong Kong. *Bruce Lee: Letters of the Dragon*, edited by John Little, p. 25.

19 Jesse Glover, *Bruce Lee*, p. 12.

20 Ibid., pp. 9-12.

21 See Jesse Glover, *Bruce Lee*, title page, and p. 15, which refers to a conversation with Bruce about Yip Man in the "latter part of 1959," and p. 12, describing the demo as having been at an annual Seafair event.

22 The January 8 diary entry is actually hand-dated "1961 Fri," but since January 8, 1961 was a Sunday rather than a Friday (January 8, 1960 was a Friday), and since the diary's first page is dated December 31, 1959, it appears that Bruce entered the wrong year for the first few entries of 1960.

23 Jesse Glover, *Bruce Lee*, pp. 17-18.

24 Bax, *Number One*, pp. 190-191; Jesse Glover, *Bruce Lee*, p. 17.

25 Bax, *Number One*, p. 180; Jesse Glover, *Bruce Lee*, p. 18.

26 Jesse Glover, *Bruce Lee*, pp. 18 and 40.

27 According to Bruce's diary, he and Jesse and Fook Yeung went to the YMCA on February 6, 1960 where he met Taky. Taky and others there apparently asked Bruce to teach them some *gung fu*. Subsequent entries for February also mention practicing judo with Taky and that he was "[I] earning some judo." He also began teaching Taky some *gung fu* at the YMCA. In addition to Jesse and Taky, Bruce also learned some judo from Fred Sato. Glover, *Bruce Lee*, p. 49.

28 Bax, *Number One*, p. 43.

29 Jesse Glover, *Bruce Lee*, p. 37. Bruce also stammered. Ibid., p. 66. A diary entry of Bruce's noted that he stuttered due to his being too concerned with making a mistake. He resolved to say what he wanted without worrying about pronunciation or grammar. Diary entry for January 21-22, 1960. Although Bruce spoke English fluently then, it was his second language that he learned in school, and was British English.

30 Bax, *Number One*, pp. 77, 143, 159 and 160.

31 E.g., see Bax, Disciples, Jim DeMile interview, p. 116, for his opinion of Bruce's fighting ability. Ibid., p. 121, discusses the reason for their break-up.

32 The ten students were Jesse, Skip Ellsworth, Pat Hooks, Howard Hall, Charlie Woo, Taky Kimura, LeRoy Garcia, Tak Miyabe, Jim DeMile and John Jackson. Ed Hart was Bruce's second student, but was in New York for a few months at the time. Bax, *Number One*, p. 225; Glover, *Bruce Lee*, p. 47; Little, *Letters of the Dragon*, March 1961 letter to Ed Hart in New York, p. 27.

33 Little, *Letters of the Dragon*, May 1961 letter to Ed Hart in New York, p. 28.

34 Diary entry for February 3, 1960. He gives no details. Jesse does not mention any particular encounter Bruce had around this time, but does recall Bruce's mention of an argument with a cook at Ruby Chow's, where the cook threatened him with a meat cleaver. Bruce dared the man to take a swing and the man backed off. Perhaps this was the "scrap" Bruce refers to. Glover, *Bruce Lee*, p. 17.

35 The name of Bruce's challenger has variously been given as either "Uechi" or "Yoichi (or Yoiche) Nakachi." In Bruce Thomas, *Bruce Lee: Fighting Spirit*, pp. 44-45, and Lee and Campbell, *The Dragon and the Tiger*, vol. 1, pp. 209 et seq., the challenger is just called "Uechi." But neither cites any source for that name, and it is the minority reference. I don't have a memory of the name from when I heard the story recounted after joining the class. It is possible that the name "Uechi" used in some accounts comes from a garbling of "Yoichi." The name "Yoichi (or Yoiche) Nakachi" appears as the challenger's name in the majority of renditions, but that name too is hard to track back to its source. In his own book published in 1976, Jesse Glover just referred to him as the "Karateman." E.g., see his *Bruce Lee*, pp. 41-45; likewise, in Paul Bax's *Disciples*, published in 2006. In Paul Bax's compilation of Jesse's letters and postings on an online forum, *Number One*, published in 2016, Jesse also mostly referred to the "Karate man" (e.g., pp. 40, 55, 102, 213 and 217), but at least once, at p. 210, referred to a "Yoiche [sic] Nakachi" as the karate man. "Yoiche" is most likely a misspelling of "Yoichi", and Charles Russo also uses that misspelling of the name (Russo, *Striking Distance*, pp. 67-68), citing some of the foregoing sources. A Google search turns up a practitioner of *kenpo karate* named Yoichi Nakachi, who was in Seattle around the same time and who ostensibly met Bruce, but a review of his on-line particulars suggests that he may not have been the guy who fought Bruce. One self-proclaimed student of Jesse's, in an on-line posting, has claimed that Jesse kept the name of the challenger secret for many years, before finally revealing it as "Yoiche [sic] Nakachi." https://darkwingchun.wordpress.com/2010/01/14/bruce-lee-the-karate-man-and-jesse-glover/. But I am dubious. Because of the uncertainty, I will simply refer to the challenger as the "karate man."

36 See Glover, *Bruce Lee*, pp. 42-45, and Bax, *Disciples*, interview with Jesse Glover, pp. 30-31, for Jesse's rendition of the fight and his comments on the challenger.

37 Ed Hart confirms this. Bax, *Disciples*, Ed Hart interview, p. 39.

38 Glover, *Bruce Lee*, p. 92.

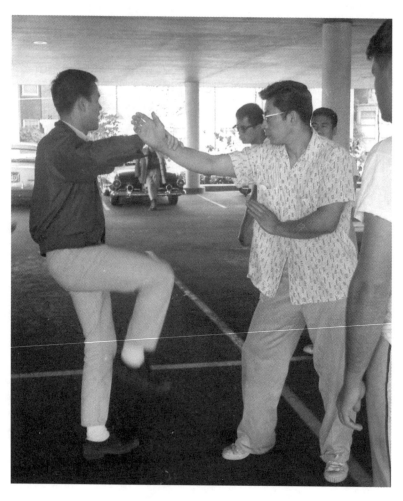

Bruce and Taky, Blue Cross Parking Garage, Seattle, circa late 1961/early 1962
Courtesy of David Tadman

CHAPTER 3
Seattle Classes

T HE WEEK FOLLOWING my encounter with Bruce at *Bon Odori*, I hitched a ride to his *gung fu* class with Jacquie Kay's younger brother, Roger. Roger was only thirteen, too young to drive, so his father took him to practice. By then, Bruce had graduated from Edison and started attending the University of Washington.

The classes then were held once or twice a week in LeRoy Garcia's back yard. LeRoy lived on the east side of Lake Washington, the long lake along Seattle's eastern border, in a log cabin he had assembled not long before. My memory is of an unpaved road or alley and a back yard that was more dirt than grass. He was a year or so older than Bruce; most of the other students were even older. LeRoy gave Bruce his first gun and taught him how to shoot it with some other students, but I don't recall any mention of that.[39]

There were ten or twelve students altogether, among whom I recognized the three who had helped give the demonstration in Chinatown: Jesse Glover; Taky Kimura, a Japanese-American in his early thirties, as husky as Jesse; and Skip Ellsworth, a white guy who towered over them both.

Jesse impressed me immediately as a laconic, no-nonsense dude, tough and fast. Then only 26, to me (aged sixteen) he seemed a lot older. I knew he was a judo practitioner (by then a black belt[40]), and he had a tattoo on the back of one hand, as I recall between his thumb and index finger, which someone told me was a "pachuco" tattoo (a cross with dots signifying crimes committed, used by Chicano gangs in California). The tattoo made him seem even tougher. I never asked him about the tattoo, or heard anyone mention it. Since Jesse was (as far as I knew) a Seattleite, and there was no Chicano gang culture to speak of in Seattle then, I had my doubts. But in my mind it served to heighten his aura of quiet lethality.[41]

The rest of the class was also multi-racial: Jim DeMile (who was part Filipino), Ed Hart, Tak Miyabe, Charlie Woo and several others. Most had some background in the martial arts, mainly judo or boxing, before running across Bruce. At the time, I thought nothing about the racial makeup of the group. It was just like any class I attended at Garfield High School.

That first class I watched was a typical one. Everyone wore regular street clothes, albeit comfortable ones. Only two formalities were observed. The classes started and ended with a stylized salutation to Bruce as the teacher, which he returned. And during class he was addressed as *Sifu* (Teacher or Master), even though he was younger than all of the students except Roger.

For the salutation, the class formed up in several rows and faced Bruce. They bowed and then executed the salutation with a flourish, fists starting at their sides, hands rolling out in front as they stepped forward to a sort of ready stance, then stepping back and reversing the hands to the starting posture. Bruce executed the same salutation as he faced the class, without the bow. Brief, but elegant.

The salutation was followed by warm-up and stretching exercises, after which the class formed up into two lines facing each other and took turns practicing offensive and defensive moves. At some point, Bruce demonstrated a new technique, and then the class paired off to spar. Sparring was at full speed and power, with no gloves or protective gear. Students were expected to aim their punches and kicks to fall short of their target by an inch or so, in case the opponent failed to block in time. As I saw later, sometimes accidents happened.

The class also practiced a few minutes of what was called meditation. The students adopted the horse stance, with their hands cupped palms-up below the abdomen, eyes closed, and concentrated on breathing deeply, inflating the stomach rather than the chest. I remember Bruce saying later that such meditation technique could develop qi[42] which in turn could produce great power in one's strikes. But he also mentioned that that could take years of practice, if not decades. His punching power didn't seem to depend on his qi, or at least any qi developed in that manner. To me, the few minutes of "meditation" seemed perfunctory, mildly intriguing but not particularly relevant to the rapid development of fighting skills.[43]

The class lasted about an hour and a half. When it ended, I was just as enthralled. I let Bruce know that I was still interested in joining the group. He nodded and said okay. At sixteen, I would be the youngest in the class next to Roger, and the only other student younger than Bruce.

THE DECISION TO join the class, however, required me to make an unpleasant choice.

The boxing lessons I had taken since grade school were

held on Thursday evenings, the same night as the *gung fu*. They were conducted in the basement of a Congregational church on Seattle's Capitol Hill by Walter Michael, whom his students and everyone else called Cap. The boxing classes were free, and open to anyone who walked in off the street, including street gangs who occasionally strolled in to scope it out and challenge some of the regulars.

Cap was a proficient martial artist in his own right, a former professional boxer. Although then nearly sixty, he could still handle any of his students with ease. His career spanned an era when professional boxers fought every week to earn a living. He also had quite a few tricks up his sleeve which were not sanctioned by the Marquis of Queensbury rules.

By then, boxing had been a huge part of my life for the past six years. Cap had been a mentor as well as a coach. I am indebted to him for first showing me how to take care of myself, for giving me the ability to distinguish competence from bluster, and the confidence to deal with dicey situations.

As a kid, my family had moved around a lot. I went to kindergarten in New Haven, first grade in Morristown, New Jersey, second and third grades and part of fourth in two different schools in the Bronx. Partway through the fourth grade we moved to Seattle and I finished fourth grade at one school, then switched for fifth grade to Madrona Elementary School when we bought a house in the Madrona neighborhood. Altogether, six different schools in six years. I perpetually seemed to be the new kid on the block.

In addition, since kids in New York started school earlier than New Jersey then, when we moved to the Bronx halfway through my first grade, I was jumped ahead into the second grade to be with kids my own age. When we moved to Seattle a few years later, we discovered that kids in my class were the same age as kids in New

Jersey, rather than those in the Bronx. But it didn't seem to make sense for me to drop back a grade at that point, so I stuck it out.

Then we moved to Madrona and to an elementary school that was half white and half black, with a few Asians thrown into the mix, a tougher school than I had attended before. I started the fifth grade there not only as the new kid on the block, but also a year or so younger (and smaller) than most of the other kids in the class.

A number of the kids boxed with Cap every Thursday. The frequent uprootings over the past few years had made me somewhat independent; but the need to constantly make new friends also made me conscious of ways to fit in to each new environment. I quickly determined that boxing would help on both scores, especially after getting thrown in a pricker bush one afternoon during an encounter with a classmate on the way home from school. I boxed every week through the end of my junior year of high school, developing a modicum of skill and gaining a lot of confidence, all of which I owed to Cap.

So it was a difficult decision to walk away from the Thursday boxing classes. In the end, however, the lure of Bruce's *gung fu* won out. It seemed to be a more complete approach to the martial arts than boxing was, using all parts of the body as potential weapons, without any limits on the method for prevailing over one's opponent in a real fight. And the insight into a whole new culture that it provided was a bonus.

I never lost my love for boxing, or my appreciation for its science. It did not seem at all odd to me when Bruce, a few years later, began to study films of some of the classic boxers, watching them over and over and mining them for practical insights to perfect his own approach to the martial arts. He would play films of Jack Dempsey, Joe Louis, Sugar Ray Robinson, Archie Moore and Muhammad Ali, among others, and comment on the moves to me or my brother Mike, who was also a boxer. (I later met and observed Muhammad Ali during the course of two different business dealings. The first occasion was while I worked in a law firm in Tokyo, in the spring of 1972, about six months before the last time I saw Bruce. Ali was also an iconic figure, similar to Bruce in a number of ways. Although they never met, I think they would have gotten along.)

But at that point in my life, in the summer of 1961, I was drawn whole-heartedly into the world of *gung fu*.

ALTHOUGH I WAS impatient to get right into the fighting techniques, the first thing I had to learn in Bruce's class was the salutation. Since it was as elaborate as an intricate dance step, it took a little time until I could execute it effortlessly. I also had to learn the *bai jong* (ready stance, with the right hand forward), so that I would have a platform to deliver the fighting techniques.

I was able to immediately participate in the various warm-up and strengthening exercises. As a skinny teenager who boxed reasonably well, I thought I was pretty flexible. I quickly realized, however, that I wasn't particularly flexible in the ways that mattered for *gung fu*. The stretches were designed mainly to loosen and strengthen the ligaments and tendons behind the knees and at the elbows, very important for the snapping kicks and punches. Otherwise, one could easily hyper-extend and tear an elbow or knee ligament.

The main exercise to stretch the tendons behind the knees was to have a partner hold your outstretched leg at hip height with one hand and press down on your knee with the other, while you grabbed your calf and attempted to touch your forehead to your knee and hold it there without bending your leg. At first I couldn't bring my head within a foot of my knee with the leg in that position, and even doing that made the tendons underneath the knee feel like they were being detached from the bones. But every night at home I would put each leg in turn up on the dining room table and bob my torso up and down with the leg straight out, until finally after several weeks I was able to touch my head to my knee and hold it there. At the time, I assumed the leg stretches were standard Wing Chun stretches, not realizing that Bruce himself had only developed such flexibility a year or so before.[44]

The other exercises I remember were also intended to limber us up. There were frog hops, where we would squat and proceed to hop like a frog around in a big circle; and an exercise where we would extend the arms straight out with the palms facing outwards and stretch the elbow joints, then raise the arms slowly up above our heads, interlock the fingers with the hands rotated upwards and stretch the elbows again. Other exercises included rotations of the neck in circles, and a form where we used the *gung bou* ("bow stance") to pivot the hips and waist and upper body as far in each direction as we could while keeping the legs in the same position. We also used *gung bou* for a kicking exercise. We would swing the back leg up at full extension in a long arc to head height, then slap the opposite palm against the inside of the foot. Since we never used that particular kick in actual fighting techniques, presumably the exercise was mainly for the purpose of stretching the various tendons and ligaments around the hips.

Many sports use stretching exercises to warm up before a practice or a game, to minimize muscle pulls and other injuries. However, the *gung fu* exercises went beyond just warming up; they seemed designed to build up the strength and resilience and enhance the extension of the tendons and ligaments that anchored the muscles, rather than the muscles themselves. None of the exercises seemed aimed at building up muscle strength *per se*, or endurance.

The unstated premise appeared to be that the muscles would take care of themselves if their foundation was strong.

Bruce's own view of training changed over the years, and he later engaged in weight training and ran for endurance, but he didn't over-do it to the extent that he sacrificed speed or flexibility.[45] One thing that struck me when I returned to the school in Seattle that was directly descended from Bruce's, run by Taky Kimura, several years after Bruce's death, was the change in the warm-up and conditioning exercises. Some of the same ones were used, but in addition there was a heavy emphasis on push-ups and sit-ups.

―――――――

AFTER THE EXTENSIVE warm-up and conditioning exercises, the classes in 1961 practiced techniques. For some of them, like the basic straight punch, we might practice them all facing Bruce (or one of the assistants who Bruce sometimes had lead the class). We would snap out a hundred straight punches, left-right, left-right, as fast as we could, starting with both fists held one above the other around the solar plexus, then punching with the upper fist straight out to full extension, bringing it back below the other fist, then punching with the second fist, and so on.

For most of the techniques, however, we formed into two lines, facing each other. If we were practicing kicks, the first person in one line would count out to ten in Cantonese and the whole line would kick to the count while the second line blocked the kick, after which the lines would switch offense and defense. There were two main kicks we practiced this way. One was the straight kick, delivered by the lead foot to the opponent's groin, which the opponent blocked with a palm slap to the top of the midfoot. The second was the side kick, aimed at the opponent's side, which the opponent blocked with a sweeping forearm. Although we aimed the kicks to land a few inches in front of the groin (in the case of the straight kick) or to the side (in the case of the side kick), it was important for the defenders to block sharply, both for the practice and in case of a miss.

The kicks could be aimed at other parts of the body—for instance, the straight kick could be aimed at the knee or shin—but we practiced kicking to the groin so that the defender could practice blocking. (A kick to the knee or shin couldn't be blocked the same way; in combat, one needed to stay out of range, then close the distance before such a kick could be delivered.) There were also other kicks we learned (such as a kick using the rear foot, delivered to the knee, and a double kick which started with a straight kick to the groin, then rolled into a higher kick to the head when the groin kick was blocked, as well as others), but we didn't practice them as much.

We also practiced hand techniques in two lines, each line alternating attack and defense. After each side had practiced both, those on one side would move down one place, so each person could work out with opponents of varying sizes and speeds and levels of ability.

The basic hand techniques we practiced this way almost every day were *paak sau*, *laap sau* and *chaap choi/gwa choi*. For techniques where the English translation was obvious, like for the side kick or straight punch, Bruce would use the English equivalent. But for the techniques where the English translation was not evident, such as the three hand techniques just mentioned, he would use the Cantonese terms, which we all learned.

Paak sau literally means "slapping hand." With both rows standing in the basic Wing Chun stance, the attacker would use his left hand to slap his opponent's leading (right) forearm aside and at the same time deliver a straight right punch over the opponent's defense. The defender would block the straight punch with his open left hand.

Laap sau means "pulling hand." As its name implies, the attacker uses his lead (right) hand to grab the opponent's lead wrist, pulling him forward and off balance while simultaneously delivering a straight punch with his left hand. The defender would block with his left.

Chaap choi/gwa choi was a combination technique, a knuckle fist (*chaap choi*) delivered under the opponent's lead arm to the ribs, followed by a back fist (*gwa choi*) to the jaw or temple when the opponent blocked the first blow. The defender would block the knuckle fist with a sweep of his right arm, which the attacker would then slap and trap while delivering the back fist.

After practicing the basic techniques, Bruce would often demonstrate a new technique, or a form, which we would then practice. Sometimes he would give a talk on the philosophical or mental aspects of *gung fu*, and how it could be applied in practice.

We also learned basic *chi sau* ("sticking hand") techniques, a form of practice which is found only in Wing Chun and a few other schools, where the two opponents adopt complementary stances with their wrists and forearms literally touching each other's as they move their arms in a set pattern from which they launch attacks. The form of *chi sau* we learned had been modified by Bruce from the way it was practiced in Hong Kong, with more forward pressure;[46] and when I returned to the Seattle school in later years it had been de-emphasized.[47]

Toward the end of the class we would pair up and spar, either using *chi sau* or free style, and the various techniques we had learned. After that, we would line up and end with the salutation again. Once class was over, we no longer had to address Bruce as *Sifu*.

ALTHOUGH I DIDN'T realize it at the time, the make-up of Bruce's class was unique in the history of *gung fu*. As I discovered later, non-Chinese were not taught in Hong Kong. Likewise in Hawaii, a melting pot in every other respect, only Chinese were taught—not even other Asians were admitted to the *gung fu* schools. As far as I know, the same was then generally true in Chinatowns across the continental U.S. Certainly Ruby Chow let Bruce know that she did not approve of his teaching non-Chinese.

A few *gung fu* instructors undoubtedly taught non-Chinese before Bruce did. For example, James Lee in Oakland (no relation), who later became a close friend of Bruce's and collaborated with Bruce when he began to develop Jeet Kune Do, privately taught a Caucasian friend some of the Chinese martial arts beginning in 1958 or so, including "iron hand" breaking techniques. I met James and his friend when Bruce and I visited James on the way back from Hong Kong at the end of summer 1963. James may also have taught a few other non-Chinese around the same time.

Other *gung fu* teachers are also said to have taught non-Chinese before Bruce even arrived in the States. This may well be so. But from all I saw and heard, that would have certainly been the exception and not the rule. And I would wager that no other *gung fu* teacher up to then had taught so many non-Chinese as openly as Bruce did. Ethnic background was literally not a factor when aspiring students asked to join his class.

The fact that Bruce openly taught non-Chinese was greeted with shock and incredulity when we gave a demonstration in Vancouver, B.C. Chinatown sometime in the summer of 1962, and later when Bruce used me to give a demonstration at a *gung fu* school in Honolulu on the way back from Hong Kong in 1963. Chinese students at Yale, whom I

Early class of students, author and Jesse flanking Bruce, Seattle, circa 1962
Courtesy of the Bruce Lee Family Archive

met when I went off to college, confirmed that their *gung fu* schools only taught Chinese. And when Bruce took me along to watch him work out with his teacher in Hong Kong, I had to pretend that I was just a friend from the States, who knew nothing about *gung fu*. Even Bruce, out of respect, did not want his teacher to know that he had been teaching non-Chinese.

A year or so after we got back from Hong Kong, in Oakland, Bruce was challenged by another *gung fu* practitioner, Wong Jack Man,[48] according to one version because the Chinese community was aghast that Bruce had opened up a school and admitted non-Chinese as students. Wong apparently denied that was the reason for the match, claiming his challenge was actually a response to a general challenge Bruce had given to local *gung fu* practitioners during a demo in San Francisco Chinatown. He also later claimed that his own school was the first one in San Francisco Chinatown to operate with "open doors"—that although most of his students were Chinese, not all of them were. I can't say for certain, but I believe Wong had not yet even started his own school at that point. In any event, if Bruce was not the first to teach *gung fu* to non-Chinese, he was certainly the first one who did it on the scale he did; and the first one who reached out so widely and openly beyond the Chinese community. In Bruce's case, the vast majority of his students were non-Chinese, and he made it a mission to proselytize to any audience he could get in front of.

The actual match with Wong Jack Man is still the subject of controversy as to almost every detail, from the reason it was held to the way it unfolded and its ultimate outcome. I have heard the story from Bruce, and I believe his version, for reasons I will explain in more detail in a later chapter.

The fact that Bruce himself was part Caucasian and by some accounts had problems of his own being fully-accepted as a *gung fu* student in Hong Kong may have had something to do with his attitude about teaching to anybody without regard to race. But as was obvious from the make-up of the class I joined, he literally did not care about a person's racial or economic background, or sex. If someone wanted to learn *gung fu* and was willing to work hard at it, Bruce was willing to teach them. The fact that with girls it afforded a good excuse to get up close and personal was perhaps an extra plus. Indeed, Bruce got to know his future wife, Linda Emery, when she took lessons.

The racial composition of Bruce's *gung fu* class was like the high school I attended, so I didn't think much about that. But the students, nearly all older than Bruce, with a wide array of martial arts and rough-and-tumble backgrounds, were all drawn to Bruce because of his obvious mastery and practical approach. There were black, Chinese, Japanese and white students with judo backgrounds (like Jesse Glover, Bruce's first student), and others (like Jim DeMile) with boxing backgrounds. Some were simply tough dudes who knew a lot about street fighting and recognized an approach that was more efficient and effective.

For Bruce's part, he seemed to revel in testing himself against guys who had been around the block and were bigger and rougher-looking than he was. He was confident and didn't hesitate to spar or engage in other physical contests. Although he was only 135 pounds or so then, I saw him arm-wrestle (and beat) a tough black kid who weighed over 225 pounds and who could easily bench-press his own weight. He also did a one-handed push-up with the same kid on his back. (He once did a three-finger push-up with me on his back, but I only weighed 170 pounds or so back then.)

At the time, it all seemed normal, but even then I had a glimmer that I was part of something special, that I was learning from someone who epitomized the best in the martial arts, not just in terms of technique or physical ability, but in overall approach.

———

OVER THE YEARS the location of Bruce's *gung fu* classes changed a number of times. Before I joined the class, Bruce and his first students practiced wherever they could—in public parks and playing fields and gymnasiums. Not too long after I joined, the class was relocated from LeRoy Garcia's back yard to a parking garage underneath a medical building on First Hill, across the street from where Bruce lived and worked, at Ruby Chow's Restaurant.

The parking area took up the entire ground level of the structure, which covered a half block or so. The multi-storied building over the parking area protected us from rain, but there were no walls. The building rested on thick columns spread throughout the parking area, like a longhouse on stilts, so in the wintertime it was as cold as the rest of the outdoors. At the times we practiced, on

Practice in Blue Cross Parking Garage, Seattle, circa late 1961/early 1962
Courtesy of David Tadman

Thursday evenings and weekends, there usually weren't too many cars parked in the garage, so we had plenty of room to spread out. And the price was right—I am confident that Bruce did not pay any rent for the use of the space. Ruby Chow's Restaurant, as well as the building with the parking garage where we practiced, has long since been torn down and redeveloped. The parking garage is now part of the Swedish Hospital complex.

Sometime during the next year the class moved again, to a run-down space in Seattle's Chinatown where a Szechuan noodleshop is today. The indoor space was marginally warmer than the open-air garage and anything but spacious. If Bruce paid any rent, it probably wasn't much. Later, the class moved to a basement location a few blocks away. (Underneath Chinatown—and the part that used to be "Japan Town" before World War II, and had been repopulated mainly

Practice in Blue Cross Parking Garage, Seattle, circa late 1961/early 1962
Courtesy of David Tadman

with Japanese after the war—was a "city" of basements, many of which were interconnected with tunnels. One time in high school I was with a group of Japanese-American friends who had a party in a basement under a Japanese restaurant, drinking beer and watching inappropriate movies. I guess we had been making too much noise, because the cops showed up and began to shine flashlights through the front door of the restaurant. We panicked and dispersed through the tunnels, leaving one friend who was too drunk to walk hidden behind a pile of empty *shoyu* (soy sauce) barrels. I emerged a block or so away from the restaurant in a different building, unmolested by the police.)

I believe the basement in Chinatown was when he started calling his school the Jun Fan Gung Fu Institute (Jun Fan being his given name in Chinese).

ENDNOTES

39 LeRoy says he taught Bruce how to shoot with a .357 pistol, and later gave him a .25 automatic. See also Glover, *Bruce Lee*, p. 66; Bax, *Number One*, p. 36; and Bax, *Disciples*, interview with Skip Ellsworth, p. 53.

40 Little, *Letters of the Dragon*, May 1961 letter to Ed Hart, p. 28.

41 Later, I found out that Jesse grew up in Seattle but moved to California when he was fifteen, before he joined the Air Force and moved back to Seattle after his discharge. Glover, *Bruce Lee*, pp. 6-7. LeRoy Garcia told me recently that Jesse was indeed exposed to Chicano gang culture in East L.A., becoming a "gang-banger" for a while.

42 *Qi* is the *pinyin* spelling for *ch'i* (literally "air" or "breath," but as a Taoist concept referring to the energy flow or life force)—the spelling using the Wade-Giles romanization system for Mandarin that was wide-spread throughout most of the 20th century. Many of the spellings usually seen for common Mandarin words still use that system—such as *kung fu* and *t'ai chi* (rendered *gongfu* and *tai ji*, respectively, in *pinyin*). Generally, if not otherwise specified, I have used the *pinyin* spelling for Mandarin words, but I am not always consistent. If the word is more familiar to Western readers using the Wade-Giles spelling—e.g., *t'ai chi* (rather than *tai ji*)—I sometimes use that.

43 Linda confirms that he didn't practice the breathing meditation that was taught in class much himself. In her words, he was more into "meditation in action." But he did quiet time with himself "just fine," reading and thinking about what he had read or observed or planned to do.

44 According to Jesse, when he first tried to develop a focused kick, Bruce found he couldn't touch his head to his knees. It took him a couple of months of stretching to be able to do so. Glover, *Bruce Lee*, p. 58.

45 Jesse Glover has written that at one point Bruce bulked up to over 160 pounds, but then took it off because the extra weight slowed him down. Bax, *Number One*, p. 176. Jesse called things exactly as he saw them, so his words hold a lot of credibility in my book, but I've never heard of that

elsewhere and never saw Bruce at that weight myself. Linda says he was never that heavy, and that even 145 (his maximum weight per another source) would be a "stretch." A chart he kept after he started weight training, depicted in Linda's *The Bruce Lee Story*, p. 71, shows him at 140 pounds in May and July of 1965.

46 According to Jesse Glover, Bruce began applying more forward pressure when working out with him and other larger Americans, and also added more modifications to penetrate the *chi sau* of the senior students in Hong Kong whose abilities in that regard were still superior to his when he left Hong Kong. Bax, *Number One*, pp. 186-187. However, a story told by Jesse suggests that the roots of Bruce's deviation from classical *chi sau* was from an incident before he left Hong Kong. Apparently Bruce practiced his own version of isometric exercises, pressing his palm up against the underside of his desk while in class, simulating one of the Wing Chun hand positions. One time his hand slipped out from the edge of the desk and flew forward, leading Bruce to think that correctly applied forward pressure could be used to his advantage in *chi sau*. Glover, *Bruce Lee*, p. 27.

47 Bruce had moved beyond *chi sau*, partly because he found that it was ineffective against much larger opponents, such as Kareem Abdul-Jabbar. Instead, he developed himself to the point that he could close the gap and strike cleanly without making contact with the opponent's hands or arms. Bax, *Number One*, p. 187, and Glover, *Bruce Lee*, p. 34.

48 I have rendered particular Chinese names as they usually appear in articles and books, rather than using a consistent word-order. In Chinese, the surname comes first, as in the case of Wong Jack Man (Wong Jak Man), "Wong" being the surname. In the case of Gin Foon Mark (Mak Gin Fun), however, his surname ("Mark") generally appears last in the articles and books I have seen, using the Western convention, so I follow the same convention when referring to him.

CHAPTER 4

The Roots of Bruce's Style

UNG FU IS a generic name encompassing scores of Chinese martial arts schools and their offshoots. The term itself literally means something like "skill" or "achievement through effort," and can also be applied to other skills, such as cooking or carpentry. My recollection is that Bruce himself translated *gung fu* as "work." The fancier term for martial arts is *wu shu* in Mandarin.

The *gung fu* Bruce taught back then was not just Chinese martial arts in general. It was a specific school of *gung fu* known as Wing Chun. But even then Bruce was tinkering around the edges with his style of Wing Chun, and the way he taught it.

The different *gung fu* schools and styles are classified in various ways. Among other classification schemes, the schools are sometimes categorized according to their religious origin (Buddhist or Taoist), or main application (kicking, hitting, wrestling or grappling), or as being either "internal" or "external" (initially concentrating on exercises that develop "internal" qualities like balance, grace and relaxation, as opposed to strength and fighting techniques).

There were also a number of styles which mimicked the perceived movements of various animals, such as the Praying Mantis, the White Crane and the Drunken Monkey.

Many of the schools were derived from techniques developed by the fighting monks at the Buddhist Shaolin Temple. The history of the Shaolin Temple, located in China on Mount Song in Henan province, goes back to the fifth century. It has become synonymous with the martial arts, and is also credited with being the birthplace of Zen Buddhism. (The wandering monk in the TV series *Kung Fu* was depicted as a Eurasian who had studied at the Shaolin Temple. The part was one which Bruce was made for. When he was living in Los Angeles and trying to break into Hollywood he did everything he could to land the part, but it was given to David Carradine, supposedly because American audiences then were not willing to accept an Asian lead actor.)

Bruce talked of "hard" and "soft" schools, *t'ai chi* being a prime example of the latter. We were also introduced to "hard" schools such as *choi lei fat (choy li fut)*, with its powerful whirling roundhouse punches, and *hung ga (hung gar)*. Bruce's classification is similar to the "internal" versus "external" dichotomy sometimes used, but he seemed to use the hard/soft distinction a little differently. For instance, *t'ai chi* is the epitome of the "internal" schools, with its practice of forms in slow motion and emphasis on internal *qi* (the internal "flow of energy"). The various Shaolin styles, on the other hand, with their emphasis on power and explosive movements, are usually thought of as "external." However, although Wing Chun was derived from Shaolin styles, Bruce clearly considered it to be a "soft" school, in that sense similar to *t'ai chi*. In any event, most schools have definite elements of both "external" and "internal," hard and soft.

In Hong Kong, Bruce had observed and perhaps informally learned different styles of *gung fu* before he settled on Wing Chun, including *t'ai chi* (which his father practiced), and learned some Praying Mantis forms. He also fought against students of other styles. During class, he introduced different schools in lectures so we got a glimpse of the variety that was out there, sometimes with commentary about their strong points and weak points. I remember him demonstrating *choi lei fat* moves, which he said (and as shown by him) were very powerful, with whipping roundhouse punches and back fists delivered with a twisting upper torso. According to Bruce, it was very effective for fighting more than one opponent, and was difficult to attack and defend against. But, as he also pointed out, in some of the moves, the back of the head was sometimes exposed when the opponent attacked with a roundhouse, then turned the body to follow up with a back fist.

In the case of the Praying Mantis and *t'ai chi*, Bruce also demonstrated them through their forms (a stylized sequence of moves used to practice different techniques, as if against an imaginary opponent).

———————

I REFERRED TO the "roots of Bruce's style" in the title of this chapter, but Bruce would have taken objection to calling his approach a "style." He often remarked that the styles as practiced by various *gung fu* schools were "starched classicism." He believed they were too rigid in their approach and techniques, and espoused a "way" (the *Tao*) that transcended style. But the roots of his approach were in a particular style.

Bruce could demonstrate forms and moves from other schools with ease and panache, but it was Wing Chun which he learned in Hong Kong from Yip Man. One of the "soft" schools (using Bruce's description), it had taken its name from a woman, Yim Wing Chun, who is credited with developing this particular style some three hundred years ago.

According to legend, Yim Wing Chun was a beauty who often found herself fending off the attentions of unwanted suitors. Some of them were particularly obnoxious, and she asked a nun at the famous Shaolin Temple, Ng Mui, to teach her something she could use to keep them at bay. Ng Mui supposedly combined elements of several Shaolin styles that she thought could be effectively employed by Yim Wing Chun to solve her particular problem, which has been passed down in its present form as the Wing Chun school. Several other *gung fu* schools also trace their lineage back to Ng Mui.

Bruce never expounded on the origins of Wing Chun that I recall. In fact, I recall him only mentioning once or twice in passing that it was started by a woman. But in my mind, its origins perfectly explained the overall characteristics of the style. Although the "hard" and "soft" dichotomy of the various schools can be somewhat misleading, the Wing Chun style did seem to epitomize a softer approach.

The Wing Chun blocks were deflecting, rather than the "hard" blocks that met blows with a rigid barrier. Even when a kick or punch was met head on, it was often with an open palm which absorbed the strike like a spring rather than a solid wall. The system was also designed to inflict damage on soft targets, such as the knee, groin, temple or eyeballs, which diminished the advantage of brute muscular strength.

Yet to characterize Wing Chun as "soft" is valid only to a point. Soft did not mean weak. Anyone who has seen Bruce demonstrate his famous "one-inch punch" understands the tremendous power his punching technique could generate.

There were other characteristics of Wing Chun which also appealed to me as a teenager, and still do today. It emphasized straight punches which could deliver focused power with an arm which was already half-extended. It capitalized on a straight line being the shortest distance between two points, as well as the fact that the starting point was already halfway to its target. In contrast, some of the harder schools used punches that started from the waist or shoulder, at least as they were often practiced in class, or which were delivered with roundhouses or other curving trajectories. Even the boxing jab, an efficient punch which was my staple when I boxed, was in a subtle way not as straight as a Wing Chun punch. In particular, the Wing Chun punch, delivered with the elbow facing down and slightly in, used an inner line which was slightly shorter than the jab, where the elbow rolls up and outward.

When I first met him, Bruce apparently already had adjusted his Wing Chun stance and techniques in subtle ways to incorporate elements of the Praying Mantis style. In later years, Bruce incorporated other punches and techniques, such as the hook derived from the boxing movies he watched, which he realized was very effective in certain close-up situations where the straight punch was not viable. But the core of his approach remained Wing Chun. And to me at the time, I had found the ultimate fighting system.

———

THE BASIC STANCE taught by Bruce when I started, which he called *ding bou*, was not at all like the boxing stance I was used to. I boxed right-handed, which meant that I stood with my left side facing the opponent, my left hand in front to jab, my right (stronger hand) cocked back at shoulder height. The upper body leaned slightly forward, weight over the balls of the feet. The chin was lowered, ready to tuck under the left shoulder. The footwork was side to side, circling, as much as forward or backward.

In contrast, the stance Bruce taught was a "southpaw" stance, with the right (stronger) arm forward, elbow in, palm open and facing inward but angled up. Since one had to defend against kicks and blows below the belt as well as above, the left hand was held at waist height, palm facing down. The knees were slightly bent, as in a boxing stance, but more of the weight (seventy percent or so) was on the back (left) foot, which allowed the leading (right) foot to be raised more quickly in a kick. The torso was also held erect, centered over the back (left) leg. The knee and foot of the right front leg were turned in slightly, to protect against kicks, the heel barely touching the ground if at all.

Although one could move quickly in any direction in a *ding bou* stance, in practice there was less lateral movement than in boxing, and no bobbing or weaving. The stance was more "planted," more centered, with focus on the waist when moving. My notes from class read, "Waist—main spring of movement of body. Movements of limbs are slow & short; waist movements are free & long. Waist more important in moving. Dissolve attack with waist. Whether advancing or retreating, waist is consciously lowered downward..."

We also learned two other stances, *ma bou* (the "horse stance") and *gung bou* (the "bow stance"), but *ding bou* was the stance we mostly trained with and used when sparring.

The horse stance is a very stable stance, with legs bent and weight distributed evenly on both legs. It is the basic stance for some *gung fu* schools, and we were told that in the "old days" students in some schools for the first couple of years during class did nothing but stand in the horse position. That was not Bruce's vision for teaching *gung fu*. A shallow horse stance was used when we practiced *chi sau*. We used a deeper horse stance when we "meditated." But we didn't use the horse stance for anything else.

In the bow stance most of the weight was put on the forward leg, with the knee and foot turned in slightly and the rear leg extended straight out behind. We used this stance for several of the conditioning exercises, but not when practicing techniques or sparring.

I later learned that the *ding bou* stance we practiced in class was not the traditional Wing Chun stance, which is more square. Whether Bruce modified his stance to bring his right foot forward due to Fook Yeung or someone else or through his own reading, he apparently found it worked better for him. He also apparently tinkered more with his stance when he first started teaching in Seattle (in early 1960). But by the time I joined the class a year and a half later, we learned Bruce's *ding bou* variation as the *bai jong*, or ready stance.

In later years, no doubt in part influenced by the boxing films he studied, Bruce loosened up his stance and allowed more movement, in terms of footwork as well as his arms. He may have exaggerated it for the movies, since it looks more exciting to dance around, but he also wanted to become lighter on his feet than the traditional Wing Chun stance. By the time he fleshed out Jeet Kune Do as his trademark "style," he even held his hands more like a boxer's.

The evolution of Bruce's *bai jong* (ready stance) is succinctly shown in Tommy Gong's book, *Bruce Lee: The Evolution of a Martial Artist*. The *ding bou* of the Seattle years is illustrated by Taky Kimura, and the shift in the feet during his Oakland years by Allen Joe. The even more boxer-like stance, from when he taught Jeet Kune Do in Los Angeles, is illustrated by Ted Wong. He retained the right (strong) hand forward throughout, however.

THE PHYSICAL SYSTEM of Wing Chun was grounded in a particular philosophical outlook. Bruce often devoted time during class to expositions of the philosophy, which he placed in a Taoist context of *yin* and *yang*. With respect to the softness of Wing Chun, he was fond of saying that one should be "soft, yet not yielding; firm, yet not hard." He had a number of favorite expressions in this regard, such as "be like water: it has no shape of its own, but rather fits into the shape of its container; it is soft, yet penetrates the hardest rock; you cannot grab it or strike it."

Bruce's Wing Chun teacher, Yip Man, constantly sought to impress on Bruce that Wing Chun was not just a set of physical techniques; there was a spiritual component that was equally important. He would tell Bruce to relax and calm his mind; to learn the art of detachment—to forget about himself and follow his opponent's movements, without deliberation.

But that was easier said than done. Bruce told the story of how he took a week off to meditate on Yip Man's advice, finally giving up and sailing out in a junk into the harbor by himself to unwind. As he thought about his level of training and got mad at himself, he punched at the water. As soon as he did, he realized that the water was the essence of *gung fu*. He struck it with all his might, but it was not hurt. When he tried to grab a handful, it slipped through his fingers. Although it seemed soft, it could penetrate the hardest rock.[49]

At first, the philosophical observations, like the meditation, seemed intriguing but not particularly practical. As it developed, however, the philosophical underpinning turned out to be not merely philosophical. It could also be applied directly to enhance the physical execution of the *gung fu*.

An example was the *paak sau*, or slapping hand, the straight right punch which we practiced delivering from mid-range but which could also be delivered from further away. The punch was delivered simultaneously with a slap of the left hand to the opponent's guard, so that the punch could flow through unobstructed directly to the opponent's face. In trying to punch and slap with both hands at the same time it was easy to telegraph what was coming. Bruce taught us to calm our thoughts when facing an opponent by imagining our mind as a still pond, as flat as a mirror, and to let our *paak sau* erupt from the stillness without any forewarning. The mental image helped a lot in producing a spontaneous strike that could penetrate the opponent's defense before he could react.

Jhoon Rhee, a Taekwondo master and friend of Bruce, talks of an explosive punch he learned from Bruce that doesn't tele- graph. Rhee says he in turn taught it to Muhammad Ali.[50] I believe that the stilling of the mind was the basis for the execution of that punch.

My hand-written notes from the classes contained a number of Taoist-like admonitions:"Establish nothing in regard to oneself. Let things be what they are. Move like water, rest like a mirror, respond like an echo, pass quickly like non-existence, be quiet as purity. Those who gain, lose. Do not precede others, always follow." But they also contained a wide range of other information.

One day Bruce might explain the proper stance or way to breathe. Another day he might talk about rules and etiquette (including,"Follow advice of teacher. Treat him with great respect... Conduct yourself [in accordance with the] principle[s] of *gung fu*, by showing forbearance and gentleness in dealing with people."). He gave instruction in the proper way to practice a form;[51] specific requirements for different body parts;[52] techniques for lengthening an opponent's reaction time (such as by moving when he is off balance, or inhaling, or is focused on one movement; by presenting him with combined stimuli, such as hand and foot at the same time; or throwing him mentally off-balance by yelling or clapping); and the correct terminology for various techniques.

My notes also list the terms for ten different punches (*gwa choi*, or back fist; *pek choi*, or hammer fist; *cheun choi*, a straight punch; the roundhouse *sau choi*; and others) and various other kinds of strikes.

OVER THE YEARS, Bruce constantly worked on a conceptual framework for the martial arts, an organic holistic approach he came to call Jeet Kune Do. Jeet Kune Do could be translated as "The Way of the Intercepting Fist," *Do* or Way being the same character as the Tao in Taoism or the *do* in *judo*. But he thought of it not as a Way that dictated your actions, but rather a Path that you traveled for your whole life.

Bruce liked to make fun of the way *gung fu* was taught by most practitioners in those days. In his view, each *gung fu* school jealously guarded its secret techniques and promoted its style as the ultimate in martial efficacy, to the point of valuing style over practicality, form over substance. He was impatient with the rigidity of the traditional *gung fu* schools, and derided the *gung fu* practitioners who, he said, sometimes went down to Thailand and were soundly beaten by tough Thai boxers who engaged in practical training. In his own classes, he tried to strip away the unnecessary and teach techniques in a way that could be used in real-life situations.

He ultimately determined that Wing Chun, while a formidable and highly practical fighting system in many respects, was itself still a system which had its own limits. But this gradual evolution in his thinking and approach only became apparent to me once I went away to college and returned periodically on vacation after months away from the weekly classes. And even as he evolved, Wing Chun remained as a core to his Jeet Kune Do.

ENDNOTES

49 Linda Lee, *The Bruce Lee Story*, pp. 37,39.

50 Jhoon Rhee, *Bruce Lee and I*, pp. 131-132.

51 "Give up all thoughts. Set eyes forward to spot just in front of outgoing hand. Imagine opponent to be in front of you. . . Close mouth. Breathe with nose. Press tongue against palate. Set shoulders down. Lower elbows, straighten head. Keep chest & back in natural position. Loosen waist. Do not force strength."

52 E.g., "Trunk—chest suck in, back raise up. Allows breathing into stomach. (The above posture does not mean hunchback. Be natural.) Chest muscles [should] be relaxed completely; breathing regulated. . ."

CHAPTER 5
A Year of Revelations

T HE SIXTIES WERE a time of ferment, but in Seattle in 1961 it was not yet clear how profound the winds of change would be. Jimi Hendrix, who attended Garfield High School before he dropped out (a few months before I met Bruce), had not yet made a name for himself; and drinking fountains and other public facilities were still segregated in the South. A *sansei* (third-generation Japanese-American) friend, who joined the army right out of high school and was posted to a base in Alabama, regaled me with stories about hopping up and down on one leg while trying to decide whether to use the restroom for whites or the one for blacks. He said he went with army buddies to both white and black bars and night clubs, but the only time he was asked to leave was in a black bar. When he protested that he wasn't white, the bartender said, "I don't know what you are, man, but I don't want no trouble with the *po*-lice."

At Garfield we congratulated ourselves on how diversified and tolerant we were, but we also realized that we were in a bubble of sorts. The Seattle housing market was segregated and the lines were strict, even though some groups were trying to break those barriers down. The city is shaped somewhat like a lopsided hourglass, pinched between Puget Sound on the west and a long lake on the east, with the downtown area climbing up the slopes along the salt water side in the middle of the waist. Blacks were confined to the Central Area, a valley between downtown and a ridge that ran along the edge of the lake to the east. Asians were for the most part confined to the same area, plus Chinatown on the southern edge of downtown and a few adjoining neighborhoods such as Beacon Hill. Private clubs in Seattle, including business and athletic clubs in the city as well as golf and country clubs on the outskirts, did not admit non-whites, or even Jews.

The catchment area for Garfield included the Central Area and Chinatown, but also some adjacent white areas along the lake, including a gated community called Broadmoor with its own golf course. Those whites living in Broadmoor who did not attend private schools (or were kicked out of them) ended up at Garfield, so the school's diversity spanned the economic as well as racial gamut. Racial tension at the school was virtually non-existent; I remember one assembly senior year at which Archie Moore spoke. He looked out over the audience and remarked that he seemed to be gazing out on a beautiful garden, "with lots of different colored flowers." What fights there were, which sometimes involved kids of different races, were usually over personal matters rather than race. And yet, race was an issue, in subtle and some not-so-subtle ways.

The sports teams and other student activities were integrated. Although the golf, tennis and ski teams were predominantly white, the football, basketball and baseball teams better reflected the diversity of the student body. And the teams were a source of pride—the football team was often the best in the city, and the basketball team often won the state tournament. But off the field, and outside of class, the kids tended to associate along racial lines. In the lunchroom students sat in informal boys' and girls' sections. In each section, blacks usually sat with blacks, Asians with Asians, whites with whites. And dating was mostly within one's own racial group—even Chinese- and Japanese-Americans rarely dated a member of the other group. This social segregation was also reflected in other institutions, such as scout troops and churches. Partly it was due to growing up in different neighborhoods, but partly it reflected shared experiences—most of my *sansei* friends, for instance, were born in the concentration camps we euphemistically called "relocation camps" set up for Japanese-Americans in places like rural Idaho and California during the Second World War.

THROUGHOUT MY ENTIRE senior year of high school and the following summer I devoted myself to *gung fu*. Every class brought something new—a new technique, a new insight into how to execute a technique more effectively. Aside from some of the Chinese students, no one else at Garfield High had heard of *gung fu*, but gradually the word spread. Many made a joke out of it, including one hulking teacher who was a former football player, Claude Wilson. He asked me if it was "like *egg foo young*" and whether it could "stand up to a good old Minnesota haymaker."

A few friends would test me, but not to a serious extent. One friend, a fairly proficient boxer, asked what *gung fu* would do against "this." He was standing close to me and without further warning unleashed a flurry of punches to my head and body. Without thinking, I blocked the punches with various Wing Chun blocks. My friend seemed impressed, but he wasn't as surprised as I was. We didn't train against such combinations of boxing punches, and I doubt I would have employed the blocks as effectively if I had known the punches were coming, or if he had thrown a second combination.

Another acquaintance in the hallway at school pretended to attack with a club of some kind in his hand. As he neared, I snapped a straight kick to within an inch of his groin. He pulled up short and looked down at his groin area with a befuddled look on his face. Realizing that my foot was back on the ground before he even reacted, let alone blocked it, he abandoned his challenge.

The only time I came close to using *gung fu* for real that year was once when I had a minor confrontation with another student. In return for an extra-long lunch period, I was given the job of watching over one of the lines in the lunchroom. The job lasted all of fifteen minutes or so, and consisted primarily of ensuring that people didn't crowd into line.

One day a kid named Floyd, whom I knew from one of my classes but not very well, ostentatiously crowded into the head of the line. I felt I couldn't ignore it, so I asked him to move back to the end. He suggested that I make him. I told him that I was busy, but if he cared to wait until after the lunch break, I would be happy to meet him outside. He nodded and stepped out of the line.

At one point I noticed that Floyd conferred with some of his friends. A little later, as the line dwindled, I saw that he was sitting over in the girl's section, chatting up a whole table of girls. I asked a mutual friend if Floyd still wanted to continue our discussion. The friend strolled over to the girl's section to check with Floyd, then casually sauntered back. "Floyd say he let you slide," the friend reported. I later learned that when Floyd told some of his buddies that he was intending to meet me outside, the buddies let him know that I was "the dude who did all like this," imitating various karate chops. I was surprised that the word had spread so widely, but very relieved at the outcome.

EARLY ON BRUCE tapped me to participate in demonstrations which he was often asked to give in various venues. This was undoubtedly because I had more free time on my hands than many of the students, most of whom had jobs and families, rather than any particular aptitude on my part.

At any rate, the demonstrations continued apace after I joined the class. For one, we drove up to Vancouver, B.C., to participate in a pageant of some sort held in an auditorium in Chinatown in the summer of 1962, before an entirely Chinese audience. That demo may have been my first inkling that what I had taken for granted—that Bruce welcomed any student regardless of race—was an anomaly in the Chinese martial arts community.

Before we went on stage, we worked out our routine. Part of the demonstration consisted of a brief choreographed "sparring match" between me and Jesse Glover. The match involved three "rounds," refereed by Bruce. Each round featured a few moves and counter-moves, at full speed but with punches and kicks pulled, until one of us "scored" a decisive blow. We choreographed it so each of us won one round, and then the third broke the tie. For the third round, we sparred back and forth for a bit, then Jesse threw a punch. I blocked the punch and countered with a straight kick to the groin which got through.

Jesse was Bruce's first student and much older than me, so I thought he should "win" the match. I said something to that effect but they both waved off the suggestion. It wasn't even on their list of things to be concerned about. This was just a demonstration; it wasn't real, and nobody's ego was on the line. It made an impression on me, especially since I was then so new that Bruce had trouble with my name after the demonstration when he was

★譚秀珍飾天香公主
★關文剛飾狄生
★新艷溈飾吳四姑
★曾慧徑周少平分飾狄支龍
★簡竹平飾盧陵王
★其餘角式太多恕不盡錄

情僧偷到瀟湘舘

前程萬里　四塲精華　演二小時　塲塲大戲

續演譚秀珍全部反串男角買寶玉的紅樓夢名劇

★★★★

特煩周少平反串女角飾石春
譚秀珍大唱主題曲表演寶玉逃禪偷到瀟湘

香港「義父舞」男冠軍李小龍。女冠軍林燕妮女士，乃香港名媛。對於芭蕾舞蹈更是出神入化。現爲美國知名大學學生。貌賽天仙。今能集男女冠軍同時表演。真是千載一時之機會。

↑少林詠春派國技大家
香港義父舞冠軍小李小龍先生

中西國技大家演員表
1. 李小龍
2. Taky Kimura（木村先生）
3. Jesse Glover（招　）
4. Dong Palmer（蕃馬）
5. Skip Ellsworth（士噁）
6. Jim Demele（坤昙路）
7. Roy Garcia（嫁綠亞）

少林詠春派國技大家李小龍。聯合中西技聯家大表演中國技擊。嘆觀止。

→軟骨美人曾美蓮小姐

雪美蓮小姐。乃美國著名軟骨奇人舞蹈小姐。現年十三歲。由五歲起便從名師學習。曾在美國各大城市表演。俱极得盛譽。

（益羣會）

★（定票處）振華聲藝術研究社
八號樓上　電話 MU 4-9681

Newspaper article about *gung fu* demonstration, Vancouver, B.C., August 9, 1962 being interviewed by a writer for the local Chinese paper. When I reminded him of my last name he jabbed his index finger into the palm of his left hand and repeated "PALM-er?" Much later, it dawned on me that some of the buzz surrounding the demonstration was not just Bruce's obvious competence, and not just the fact that he was teaching Chinese martial arts to non-Chinese, but that he was bringing them into the heart of the Chinese community to help give a demonstration of their own martial arts.

As a result of the trip up to Vancouver, I acquired a Chinese name. In the article in the Chinese paper about our demonstration, my last name was transcribed with two Chinese characters which in Cantonese are pronounced *Pa Ma*. As is commonly done in Chinese with foreign names, characters were chosen which approximated the sound of the name, without regard to meaning. The two characters read as *Pa Ma*, for "Palmer," literally meant "father horse."

Bruce wasn't satisfied with those characters for my last name, however. He suggested *Baak Ma*—White Horse—as having more pizzazz and being more dignified, even though the sound was not as close. He added a character for *Dak* (pronounced "duck") which literally means "virtue," as an approximation of "Doug." I have used *Baak Ma Dak* as my Chinese name ever since.[53]

AS PRECISE AS the *gung fu* moves all were, accidents inevitably happened. My most vivid memory of an accident is from sparring one time with Jesse Glover. No doubt because I subconsciously knew the kicks were being pulled, I sometimes did not pay proper attention to my blocking technique. During one session, he blasted a straight kick to my groin. I was starting to move in, and did not have my waist low enough so that my hand could properly block it. I can attest that a full-on straight kick to the groin can be profoundly arresting.

Another time we were lined up in two lines to practice various techniques, taking turns with offense and defense. By then we were working out in the covered Blue Cross parking garage near Ruby Chow's Restaurant. The particular technique we were practicing was a *chaap choi/gwa choi* combination. It was my turn to be on offense.

The first step for the person on offense was to execute a *chaap choi*, a low punch with the knuckles to the ribs of the defender. The defender was supposed to block with a downward sweep of his right forearm; the attacker then used his left arm to pin the defender's right elbow while simultaneously letting his withdrawing right hand flow into a *gwa choi*, or back fist, delivered to the head. The defender was supposed to block the back fist with the open palm of his left hand, held a little in front and to the right side of his face. The entire sequence, offense and defense, if done correctly, flowed smoothly from one move to the next.

I was paired with a big muscular judo guy who had recently joined the class, and who was well over two hundred pounds, outweighing me by thirty or forty pounds. He didn't really seem into it, however, and in fact seemed almost dismissive of the instruction he was given. When I delivered the *chaap choi*, he blocked it with a rather awkward movement of his right arm, which had the side effect of making it harder for me to execute the follow-up back fist. Despite repeated comments, he didn't seem to be trying too hard to get the block down right. As a consequence, I decided I would deliver the *chaap choi* and subsequent back fist more quickly, and pin his elbow before he could swing his right arm out and smother the development of the back fist.

There were two variations of the back fist we used. One used the entire back of the fist to strike the jaw or side of the head. The second variation used a phoenix-eye, with the bent index finger extended out to expose the middle knuckle and the thumb pressed against the side of the bent finger to make it firm. With that configuration, the blow is delivered to the temple, with the one exposed knuckle. I employed the second variation.

As I delivered my speeded-up sequence and rolled into the back fist, I realized that my partner was not getting his left hand up in time to block it. I tried to pull the blow at the last second, but my knuckle rapped his temple. I thought I had barely touched him, and started to reach out and apologize. He immediately grabbed his head, however, and collapsed against a parked car. His knees shook and his eyes crossed and uncrossed and then crossed again. Bruce strolled over and asked what had happened. When I explained, he nodded. "Be a little more careful," he said, and moved on down the line.

It was at least ten minutes before my partner could stand up straight and resume practice. Up to then the potential effect of a temple strike had been relatively academic. But the accident brought home to me how lethal some of the techniques could be. (For whatever reason, the judo guy dropped out of the class soon afterwards.)

Even Bruce himself could on occasion misjudge the distance. Once Bruce was teaching me a move called *sin jeung*, or fan palm. The move can be a counter to a *paak sau*, where the punch is trapped with the left hand and the right palm is delivered with the extended arm to the side of the opponent's head, while leaning back slightly and turning sideways. Bruce threw a punch, then casually moved his head back an inch or so to avoid my hand when I countered. But I have long arms and the tips of my fingers brushed his cheek. Even if delivered with greater speed and power, it would have caused no damage. But Bruce was surprised and clearly displeased at the miniscule misjudgment.

He frowned and muttered something about my arms being longer than he thought.

In a more serious misjudgment, a couple of years later, he almost blinded Taky Kimura. Classes were then held up in the University District, and I was home on a vacation from college. Bruce was demonstrating a punch to the whole class. He used Taky, then an assistant instructor, to demonstrate the punch. But he was facing the class to give his exposition when he actually delivered it. The punch was so fast as to be barely visible. Taky was wearing sturdy glasses, and the punch was off by a few millimeters; one of the lenses shattered in a dramatic explosion. Taky immediately grabbed his eye and bent over, without uttering a sound. Fortunately his blink reflex must have been instantaneous. He eventually picked a few shards of glass out of his eye, but there was no permanent damage. Both of them carried on as if nothing had happened.[54]

Bruce was also injured in a few accidents which occurred during the filming of his movies, including one instance where he cut his hand on a broken bottle and needed stitches. Accidents were definitely the exception, not the rule. But they illustrate the Japanese proverb that "even a monkey can fall from a tree."

THE ONLY PIECE of equipment we saw in class was a teakwood dummy called a *muk yan jong*, which Bruce used to practice his *chi sau* techniques and strengthen his forearms. The dummy consisted of a torso with three protruding arms and a lower protrusion which simulated a leg. The whole thing was suspended on a frame with a spring that would give a little when hit. Bruce pounded the dummy with violent force, but the students didn't use it much. I also recall seeing a Lone Ranger mask which Bruce suspended from the ceiling and used to practice eye jabs, but again, we didn't practice with that in class.

Traditionally, *gung fu* schools have taught techniques with various weapons, including different kinds of swords and spears. But Bruce didn't. In fact, the only weapon I recall him even showing in class was a three-section club, a weapon like a *nunchaku* but with three sections instead of two. I remember Bruce demonstrating various techniques with it, but he never taught it in class. Presumably he considered the three-section club, and even more so swords and spears, as being of little practical value in the modern world.

Bruce's older brother, Peter, was an expert fencer. Bruce apparently adapted some fencing techniques in his Jeet Kune Do, but I never saw him use a rapier or any of the Chinese swords.[55]

Later on, when he moved down to Los Angeles, he was introduced to the *nunchaku* by Dan Inosanto, a weapon he popularized in his films. I never talked to him about it, but I suspect he realized its potential as a cool weapon for his films. Once he decided to use it, he set out to master it. He quickly became an expert in its use, and made it his own. But I don't know if he ever taught it to students.

Several times in recent years, friends have sent me Internet links to footage of "Bruce" apparently playing ping pong with a *nunchaku* and asked me if it was real. Without anything to base my answer on other than the unbelievability of wielding a *nunchaku* with such accuracy—even with Bruce's reflexes and coordination—I always told them that it was a fake. I have since read online that the footage was created in 2008 (many years after Bruce's death) as a Nokia ad. But the footage was well-done, and Bruce's mesmerizing skill with the *nunchaku* made it only a very short leap of faith to believe that he was actually capable of using it to play ping pong.

In retrospect, it makes perfect sense to me that Bruce would not teach his classes how to use weapons like swords that were impractical to carry around in today's world. But I have sometimes wondered why we never learned any defensive techniques against clubs or knives. Certainly knives were sometimes used in the street fights he was familiar with, growing up in Hong Kong; and they were a weapon of choice in some neighborhoods in the United States before guns became a scourge. But we never practiced any moves to counter a knife attack. Perhaps he realized that it is very hard to defend against a proficient knife fighter, and thought that practicing defensive techniques would impart a false sense of confidence that could lead to serious injuries.

A friend and fellow *gung fu* student, Lanston Chinn, who palled around with Bruce after I went off to college, was accosted once by three toughs. One of them pulled a knife after Lanston had dispatched the other two. Lanston tore off his jacket and wrapped it around his forearm, which he used to sweep the knife aside as he closed with the attacker. I thought the move was pretty slick, and it worked well with the *gung fu* techniques he used to overcome his opponent, but he didn't learn the jacket move in *gung fu* class.

Likewise, I sometimes wondered why we never learned how to disarm someone with a gun. As mentioned earlier, a couple of Bruce's first students taught him how to shoot a gun. According to them, he was a "natural shot." But my only memory of any discussion of guns by Bruce is a time when he talked about a particular stance used by pistol-carrying highwaymen in China. I recall him standing with his left side slightly forward, his left arm held out in a sort of halting gesture, while his right hand holding the pistol next to his body at waist level. According to Bruce, it was hard to get past the left arm to take the gun away without getting shot;

whereas if the gun is held in front of you and you were too close to the other person, he might be able to knock the gun out of your hand before you could pull the trigger.

Skip Ellsworth tells of practice sessions with Bruce where he would point a cap gun at Bruce from a couple of feet away. Bruce would start with his hands in the air, but Skip was never able to pull the trigger before Bruce deflected the gun and lanced a simulated finger jab into his eyes.[56] LeRoy Garcia says Bruce could disarm him from seven feet away. But we never practiced that in class. Disarming someone with a gun is a risky business, certainly not a sure move for someone who was not as fast as Bruce.

The only other weapon I recall Bruce demonstrating was a spear. This was years later, when my wife and I visited him and Linda in Hong Kong the year before he died. He was in the process of renovating a new house in Kowloon Tong, a section of Hong Kong. Burglary was not uncommon in Hong Kong then, and even with high walls and broken glass embedded in the top surface of the wall, a determined burglar getting inside the compound was a possibility. Bruce picked up a spear he had leaning in a corner and showed us a technique to employ against an intruder. He held the spear almost like a pool cue, its tip flicking out like a snake's tongue. My recollection is that he had the spear handy in case the intruder carried a knife. Guns were rare in Hong Kong, but knives were a different matter. If anyone could hold his own against a knife, it was Bruce. But he was also practical, and in the dark even he might have had a problem.

In the only story I have heard about him confronting an actual intruder in Hong Kong, however, he used a side kick to dispatch the man, not a spear or other weapon. Apparently his adrenaline was surging; the man had to be half-carried out from the courtyard and was left leaning up against the outer wall.[57]

SOMETIME DURING THE summer following my senior year of high school, or after I left for college, Jesse dropped out of the class. I think I asked Bruce once what happened to Jesse, but got only a vague answer. Over the years I often wondered about it. I knew Jesse was still in Seattle, and teaching his own brand of the martial arts in his low-key way. We came across one another a time or two at memorial events celebrating Bruce's legacy, but never talked about it. [58]

I suspected that as an independent, free-thinking guy six years older than Bruce, it was hard for him to be part of an entourage to someone who must have seemed like a precocious younger brother. But after reading Jesse's own accounts, that may have been only part of it.

Jesse has mentioned that one of the reasons he left was because he couldn't afford the dues that Bruce had started charging. Frankly, I don't remember when he started charging dues, and it may have been after I left for college.

Other reasons given by Jesse for dropping out were that Bruce wasn't teaching the same way he was when Jesse first trained with him, and that he had started wanting everyone to call him *Sifu* during class. In any event, by all accounts they remained friends and continued to see each other from time to time.

TOWARD THE END of my senior year, I faced a decision as difficult as giving up boxing for *gung fu*. I wanted to go back East to college, and was interested in math and physics, as well as Asian languages. I applied to MIT (which was strong in math and science but also offered Asian languages) and Yale, where my father had gone. Yale was one of a handful of universities then that were known for Asian Studies. I was admitted to both, but Yale gave me a better financial package, so I accepted its offer.

I was heavily into *gung fu*. I hung out with Bruce after class and we got together at other times. Many evenings we would end up at a restaurant in Chinatown to eat, and I learned how to order some dishes in Cantonese, such as *hou yau ngao yuk faan* (oyster sauce beef and rice), which was one of Bruce's favorites. Bruce had visions of opening up additional schools and suggested that I might be able to be a teacher at one. Although the discussion about a chain of schools was just talk at that point, as graduation neared it began to sink in that by going back East I would be cutting myself off from *gung fu*. Not to mention my girl friend.

By then, however, I had no backup. Going to the University of Washington, in Seattle, would have been a logical choice, but I hadn't bothered to apply there. So, at the end of the summer of 1962 I took off for New Haven with ambivalent feelings. I was aware of the opportunity Yale afforded, but at the same time fretted that I was foreclosing an equally fulfilling life path.

ENDNOTES

53 Cantonese has competing romanization systems, like Mandarin. Many common place names and surnames use an older, more haphazard system, as exemplified by "Hong Kong" and "Kowloon" and the "Tsimshatsoi" district of Kowloon, and by Bruce's own surname, "Lee." Since Cantonese is not as widely used as Mandarin, the Cantonese spelling is not as standardized. My own notes from the days of *gung fu* class use my own seat-of-the-pants romanization, derived from the way Bruce spelled the words out, but the spelling is not consistent. I remember Bruce asking one of the (non-Chinese) students once how to spell a particular Cantonese *gung fu* term. I have elected for the most part to use the Yale system for Cantonese terms (minus the tone markers), which I like because it seems intuitively closer to the actual pronunciation for American readers. The main exceptions are place names and surnames, where I have usually stuck with the older spellings that people are used to seeing—hence, "Hong Kong" instead of *Heung Gong*, "Kowloon" instead of *Gau Lung*, and "Lee" instead of *Lei*. In the case of my own name, *Baak Ma* (for "Palmer"), in Mandarin the characters would be rendered as *Bai Ma*—the pronunciation being even less close. But I like the characters and the imagery of a "white horse," so I continue to use the name.

54 Bruce apparently later drove Taky to the emergency room to check on the eye, but that must have been after class was over. Glover, *Bruce Lee*, p. 72.

55 Matthew Polly, in *Bruce Lee: A Life*, at p. 201, states that when Bruce fenced with his brother Peter years later, Peter said that Bruce had improved so much he "could not touch him." Apparently Peter was surprised, since the last time he had seen Bruce's fencing abilities, before Bruce left Hong Kong, they were rudimentary.

56 Bax, *Disciples*, interview with Skip Ellsworth, p. 54.

57 Bax, *Number One*, pp. 142 and 183.

58 Jim DeMile and LeRoy Garcia dropped out around the same time. The three set up their own school for a while. LeRoy quotes Jesse as saying, "LeRoy sparred with everyone, Jim talked to them, and I taught them."

CHAPTER 6
A Year Away

ARRIVED IN NEW Haven as a hick from the West Coast. Virtually no one at Yale had ever heard of *gung fu*. The only students that I came across who had were a couple of Chinese students from Honolulu, one of whom had taken lessons there. His school was a "harder" one, and we sparred a few times to test out our respective styles, but neither of us was a teacher and the two different styles were difficult to practice together. I also met a kid from Salt Lake City who had studied *aikido*, which piqued my interest, but it would have been even harder to practice with him.

I had signed up for courses in physics, math, English and Chinese history, and an intensive course in Mandarin Chinese with ten hours of class a week. I tried to make the most of my Chinese classes.

One of my freshman roommates, a Jewish kid from New York City who ended up majoring in English Literature, thought I was wasting my time taking math and physics, and that taking Chinese was downright ridiculous. When the class started learning written Chinese characters, I used flashcards. He thought it was hilarious to insert a flashcard with "Fuck you!" or some similar greeting into my stack of cards when I wasn't around.

Nor was that point of view confined to fellow students. The following year I took Japanese as well as Chinese. Each sophomore was assigned to a professor who was supposed to counsel us on our course load and whatever other matters we had questions about. At the first (and only) meeting I had with my advisor, he perused my transcript and remarked on the fact that I was taking Chinese. "And Japanese, too," he said, raising his eyebrows. I allowed that I was. "What about French?" he said. I looked at him in confusion and stammered, "What about French?" He went on as if I hadn't spoken. "If you take French, you must take it at least three or four years to become proficient," he said. "And to be civilized, you must speak French, you know."

I had nothing against French; it's just that I especially wanted to learn Chinese. Since Bruce spoke Cantonese, I had wanted to take that dialect. But only Mandarin was offered then at Yale. I was mildly disappointed about that, but at least the written characters were mostly the same.

AS IT TURNED out, my freshman year at Yale was not entirely a happy one. I had some stimulating professors, and the Chinese language classes were excellent. But this was before Yale became coed. I found the all-male environment, with women brought in on buses from neighboring women's colleges for weekend mixers, to be less than enjoyable.

Sometime in the late fall I got into an altercation. I was at a party in the living room of a suite in one of the freshman dorms. It was crowded with fellow freshmen and the alcohol flowed. A kid from the suite across the hall, a member of the freshman football team, entered the room and pushed his way roughly through the crowd. I may have jostled him as he pushed past, and vaguely heard him ask someone to hold his drink. The next thing I knew he hit me and I stumbled backwards, tripping and falling onto my back. Then he was on top of me, pounding away with both fists.

Instinctively, I raised my head and tried to hug him closer with one arm, so he had less leverage to punch. I heard someone (I think the kid from Salt Lake City who practiced *aikido*) yelling, "Use your *gung fu!*" I thought to myself, "Shit, I'm on my back—we didn't learn any moves from that position." Still hugging my assailant with one arm, I reached down with my other hand and grabbed his nuts. I squeezed as hard as I could.

Suddenly he was off me. I wasn't hurt, so I scrambled up. I saw his back disappearing through the crowd and followed him into his suite across the hall. The door was open—there were several kids in that room too, part of the extended party. I stopped in the living room and looked around to see where he had gone. He emerged from one of the bedrooms and told me to get out.

As he advanced, I hit him with a left hook. He fell back, and I followed up with a straight kick to his groin. He sort of folded up, but didn't drop. One of his roommates yelled out for me to fight with my fists. I thought, *screw that*. But at that point, I hesitated. My opponent was defenseless. The side of his jaw was red from my blow. I could have stepped forward and hit him with any punch I wanted. Instead, I looked at him, then turned and walked away. That night as I fell asleep I replayed the events of the evening over and over and asked myself why I hadn't finished the job.

A day or two later I ran into the same kid on the way to a class. We were both carrying notebooks in one hand, walking in opposite directions through a narrow space between buildings. No one else was around. He slowed slightly when he saw me, but kept walking.

I slowed down too. From the expression on his face, it looked like he was wondering what I was going to do. I wondered the same thing. I regretted not finishing the job before—should I finish it now? But as he passed, I couldn't bring myself to hit him without warning, and it seemed stupid to stop and challenge him to another fight. In the end, I found myself just swinging my shoulder hard into his as we passed. He kept walking.

Afterwards, again, I felt frustrated, as if nothing had been resolved. It took me a long time to accept the fact that I lacked the killer instinct. When the adrenaline was flowing, I could dish it out. But once the heat of the moment dissipated, I found it hard to initiate an offensive move. I was a counter-puncher.

Bruce had no such problem. He had no problem throwing the first punch (or kick) if he was provoked. In his earlier years, it hadn't taken much to provoke him. By the time I met him, he still had a temper but had learned some self-control. It took a lot more provocation before he would initiate action, but sometimes he did. And in a fight, once he started, his nature was to finish it.

He was also a master at controlling a situation. He could dominate an antagonist and make him look like a fool in front of onlookers without hurting him. Even more important, he had the situational skills to handle confrontations without violence. I saw him deal with annoyances with finesse and physical mastery without harming anyone. I never witnessed the rarer times when he was provoked enough to actually strike someone.

SOMETIME IN THE late fall of 1962 Bruce drove down to Oakland to meet James Lee. He had apparently met James briefly when he first arrived in San Francisco, and gave cha-cha lessons to James's brother.[59]

Over the course of three years in Seattle some word of an upstart kid with amazing abilities had percolated down to Oakland, and James asked a friend, Wally Jay, a judo and jujitsu expert, to look the kid up when he visited the 1962 Seattle World's fair. Wally Jay was won over and reported back that the kid was impressive.

Wally Jay's report prompted James to ask another friend, Allen Joe, to look Bruce up too, when he also visited the World's fair with his family, probably sometime in the fall. After some initial skepticism, Allen Joe was also impressed by Bruce, and persuaded James to invite Bruce down to Oakland.[60]

The drive from Seattle to Oakland took about sixteen hours, and Bruce drove down by himself. He had heard of James, who had by then self-published a couple of books on *gung fu*, and sensed a kindred spirit who didn't kowtow to ossified tradition; someone who searched for practical techniques wherever he could find them. Bruce also understood that the martial arts scene in the Bay Area was a notch or two above Seattle's, both in level and extent. Perhaps he sensed a way back into it.

The meeting proved to be pivotal. Bruce and James were indeed kindred spirits. Bruce respected James's experience and advice in a number of areas, including bodybuilding, training equipment and dietary supplements. James was also proficient at breaking bricks with his hands, being able to focus his energy to break a specific brick in a stack without breaking the bricks above or below. For his part, although he was two decades older, James recognized Bruce's spectacular martial arts abilities.

Bruce returned to Seattle with the seed planted for two endeavors.[61] One was to publish his own book on *gung fu*, which James encouraged. The second was to move down to the Bay Area. By then Bruce realized that although he was a big fish in the martial arts scene in Seattle, it was a very small pond. He was confident that he could survive and even thrive as a bigger fish in a much bigger pond.

BY CHRISTMAS VACATION of my freshman year at Yale, I was eager to get back to Seattle, my girl friend and *gung fu* classes. Once home, I discovered that Bruce had made more connections at my high school. Claude Wilson, the same teacher who had asked me if *gung fu* could "stand up to a Minnesota haymaker," had invited him to give a presentation to one of his classes. Bruce, always ready to promote *gung fu*, was happy to oblige. He asked me to accompany him, since I still knew people at the school.

My younger brother Mike was then a junior. I knew a lot of his friends, as well as other students. Jacquie Kay's younger sister Sue Ann was then a senior (Jacquie being the person who initially introduced me to Bruce). Linda Emery, whom Bruce later married, was a friend of Sue Ann and also a senior. It was during one of his visits to Garfield that year that Linda first saw Bruce, while she was walking in the hallway with a girl friend.

The class we visited was made up of seniors. A group of football and basketball players sat together in the back of the room, sprawled in their chairs. I think the teacher had given up on trying to teach much to the class; inviting Bruce to give a demonstration was one of his ways to pass the time and keep them entertained. He introduced Bruce and then sat off to the side.

Bruce started off with a brief introduction of what *gung fu* was. His English was fluent, but he spoke with a slight accent and occasional stutter. The kids smirked at each other. Bruce segued into a description of different kinds of punches. He demonstrated a classic karate-style punch from the hip, and then in contrast a Wing Chun punch from the solar plexus. The punches were snappy and delivered with obvious speed and power, but the kids were too cool to be impressed. He moved on to describing a shorter punch, later known as the "one-inch punch," though I don't recall if he used that term then. He said he needed a volunteer to help with the demonstration. Of course no one volunteered, so Bruce pointed to the biggest of the kids lounging in the back, a black kid on the basketball team, and asked him to come up.

The kid strutted up to the front and casually stood in front of Bruce, sideways to the class. Bruce set up with his right arm extended to almost full reach, his open palm an inch in front of the kid's chest. The kid towered over Bruce. The jocks in the back of the class rolled their eyes. What was this little Chinese guy going to do?

Bruce made a show of getting ready to deliver his one-inch punch, then stopped. "Just a second," he said. "I think we need something." He made an even bigger show of walking past the basketball player to pick up an empty chair that was some ten feet away, then brought it back and positioned it a few feet behind the guy. Bruce walked back around to resume his original stance in front of the kid and said, "OK, I think we're ready now." He stretched his arm out again until his fingertips rested lightly on the kid's chest, the heel of his hand only an inch or two away, and asked if the kid was ready.

Up to that point the basketball player had been playing it cool, standing there rather nonchalantly. But then he turned his head as inconspicuously as he could to look at the chair Bruce had positioned a few feet behind him. He moved one of his feet back a foot or so to brace himself, just in case. The class was now sitting up, watching intently. The kid signaled that he was ready.

Bruce's fully-extended arm shimmered, his waist moving forward a bit to generate the power through the length of the arm. The heel of his hand made contact with the kid's chest and the kid was literally picked up off his feet and flew backwards, arms flailing. He landed in the chair and kept going, knocking the chair over and sliding on his back across the floor. There were audible gasps from the class. Bruce made another big show out of walking over to the kid and helping him up, dusting him off and thanking him for his assistance with exaggerated politeness. From then on, Bruce had the rapt attention of the entire class. They hung on his every word as he explained what *gung fu* was in general, and his style in particular.

This demo of the one-inch punch became a staple of Bruce's repertoire. As a consummate showman, he used it throughout his career to generate instant appreciation for his prowess. Among other instances, he used it during the 1964 Long Beach International Karate Championships, which introduced him to Hollywood contacts, and after moving down to Los Angeles with James Coburn to make him a convert.[62]

Sometime during the holidays, Bruce mentioned that he planned to go back to Hong Kong in the springtime and stay for four or five months. He asked me if I would be interested in visiting him during summer vacation. I told him I certainly would be.

———

AFTER CHRISTMAS BREAK, back in New Haven, with no *gung fu*, I threw myself back into boxing. Sometime during the winter I tore the meniscus cartilage in my right knee, stupidly trying to demonstrate a Russian Cossack dance to one of my roommates. Unfortunately, the kicking motion in such dance, at least as I was executing it, was not as controlled as a *gung fu* kick. As a result of the injury, I had to completely reinvent my boxing style.

Throughout high school I was a tall, skinny kid, 6'-2" and 165-170 pounds when I graduated. Often my opponents were stronger, and I used my jab to keep them at a distance and became a counter-puncher if they were able to press through. With my torn right knee, however, I was unable to put much weight on it; I had to keep almost all my weight on my left leg instead. Since I fought with a right-handed stance, with my left leg forward, it was hard to move backwards easily. As a result, I developed a hopping one-legged stance that could move forwards or sideways.

Yale had an intramural boxing tournament for its freshmen, and a separate one for upper classmen. The weight divisions were set up differently than professional divisions. We had an unlimited weight class, which as I recall was over 205 pounds. The next class down was called "heavyweight," which was the division I signed up for. There were several boxers of that weight, but only three freshmen signed up for the tournament, myself and two football players who hadn't turned out to box but decided to have a go at it. In the first match, the two football players faced each other while I drew a bye. One of them was the fullback on the freshman team, a black kid from Kansas City, who knocked his opponent out.

The matches were only three rounds, but each round was three minutes, and I was not in particularly good shape. When our match started, it was obvious that the fullback was in very good shape, and very strong. He was also very aggressive, with a straightforward style that kept bearing in, but I managed to keep him off balance with my jab all through the first round. This made him very frustrated, and in the second round he bore in even more aggressively. Fortunately for me, he was off balance when he rushed in, and toward the end of the round I caught him with a tight left hook that knocked him down.

But not out. In the third round, he came out blazing. I had no energy left by then. My jab had no strength. I could barely get it up in the air, and when it made feeble contact with his face it didn't slow him down at all; the force of his advance would simply collapse my left arm back up on itself, like a folding chair. I realized I needed a new strategy to survive the round. With my weight on my left foot I would lean as far back as I could when he came sailing in. I would avoid the first couple of blows, and then quickly move my body forward to meet him, muffling his swings as best I could and tying him up. The ref would move to separate us, and as the ref stepped back I would circle in the same direction, so my opponent had to chase me around the ref as he got out of the way. When my opponent caught up to me, I would repeat the same process over again. Somehow I survived, winning the first two rounds and thus the match on total points, then stumbled down to the locker room and threw up. If the fight had gone another round, I would have been killed.

I learned a lesson in that fight, about how important it was to be in shape. It was a lesson that Bruce learned a few years later in a different fight. I was lazy and hated to jog, so the lesson for me was somewhat academic. In Bruce's case, however, he took it to heart and turned himself into an even more honed physical specimen.

IN SEATTLE DURING the first part of 1963 Bruce began work on the book he planned to publish through James Lee. His scheduled trip to Hong Kong was fast approaching and he wanted to get as much done as he could before he took off. He lined up Jesse, Taky, Charlie Woo and Jim DeMile and choreographed them in photos of various techniques for the book.

Toward the end of March Bruce flew back to Hong Kong, his first time back since he had left with a hundred dollars in his pocket nearly four years before.[63] His family all turned out at the airport to welcome him home, along with family friends. He had left a rebellious troublemaker who hadn't finished high school, on a downward spiral of trouble, to venture to a foreign land he had no memories of. The family was anxious to see what kind of young man he had become. His younger brother Robert, only ten when Bruce left, was then fourteen and especially looking forward to see the older brother he idolized.

The homecoming was a major event. Bruce brought gifts for his parents, including a raincoat for his father draped over his arm complete with coat hanger, and cash for his brother and sister. Due to the success of his last movie as he left for the States, the Hong Kong media also turned out at the airport.

In short order the family realized that Bruce had made amazing strides in his physical abilities, as he demonstrated two-finger push-ups, V-ups supported only by his hands on the floor and other feats. They also recognized that he had matured quite a bit. In between the family obligations and social get-togethers, he visited various martial artists to increase his perspective of other styles. "Never Sits Still" was keeping busy.

━━━━━━

WITH BRUCE BACK in Hong Kong, the possibility of joining him there for part of the summer took on shape. One of the newer students who had joined the class after I left for New Haven was also invited. The original plan was that the two of us would rent an apartment somewhere close to where Bruce's family lived.

The other student Bruce invited was a high-school classmate of mine, Lanston Chinn, the one who had an occasion to use his *gung fu* against three punks with a knife. Lanston was a cousin of Jacquie Kay, the friend who introduced me to Bruce, but I knew him only slightly at that time. My impression of him was that he was a hood. Most of the Chinese in Seattle then lived either in Chinatown (which fed into my high school), or up on Beacon Hill (which fed into a different high school). Lanston's family lived in the heart of the Central Area, and he hung out mostly with black kids.

Lanston was a scrapper. He wasn't particularly big or strong or fast, but he had plenty of guts and had no problem taking the first swing with whatever was at hand, especially against a larger opponent. My brother Mike told me that when Lanston visited him a few years later down at Stanford (which Mike was then attending), Lanston got into an argument with a big football player at a fraternity party. Lanston backed out the door onto a patio and kicked over a charcoal grill. When the football player came through the doorway, blinded by an outdoor light behind Lanston, Lanston was holding an iron poker and about to swing it against the side of the football player's head. Mike grabbed Lanston from behind to prevent him from seriously injuring the guy. I had a similar experience with Lanston myself when I stopped him from knocking a kid who was dating his cousin through a glass door from behind.

During the last half of my freshman year, Lanston and I began exchanging letters, and made plans to room together in Hong Kong. By the time I returned to Seattle at the end of May, however, Lanston had started having random episodic seizures. Although the doctors eventually figured out how to control the seizures with a regimen of medicines, at that point it was not deemed prudent for him to take off for Hong Kong.[64]

One of Lanston's seizures occurred during the beginning of 1963, when he was sitting with Bruce and cousin Jacquie in the HUB (the Husky Union Building, the student center at the University of Washington), where they hung out between classes. When the seizure occurred Bruce took charge. He put a spoon in Lanston's mouth to prevent him from swallowing his tongue (common advice at that time for seizures) and told everyone else to stand back.

I had my own medical problem—I was still hobbling around with a torn meniscus cartilage, often with a cane. Sometimes the

Cong,

Well, it has been quite
a time since I last
heard from you.
Here's something I like
to tell you.

The water supply here is
coming to crisis — 4 hrs
a day, every other 4 days
The temperature is
around 95° and it's like
living in hell.

My plan is to hope to
leave at the end of July
So if you don't mind
coming for around a
month and then to Japan
and Honolulu. You're
very welcome to stay
in my house.
In any case, let me
know ahead of time.

man! I can't stand
the heat!

Bruce

Aerogramme from Bruce to author, spring of 1963

knee improved enough so that the cane wasn't necessary, which enabled me to box with the odd hopping strategy I adopted. But a slip on the ice or even just a twist when I rolled out of bed in the morning could set me limping again. A doctor at the Yale infirmary had prescribed a regimen of whirlpool baths and physical therapy, but told me that if the knee didn't heal by itself I would need to have an operation to remove the cartilage. I figured I could have the operation when I got back from Hong Kong, however, so I was still inclined to go ahead with the trip.

***

SINCE IT WAS now just me going, Bruce invited me to stay with his family. In a flimsy blue aerogramme used then for overseas letters, Bruce tried to prepare me for the experience:

> *"Here's something I like to tell you. The water supply here is coming to crisis—4 hrs. a day, every other 4 days [sic]! The temperature is around 95° and it's like living in hell. My plan is to hope to leave at the end of July. So if you don't mind coming for around a month and then to Japan and Honolulu you're very welcome to stay in my house."*

He ended the letter with, *"Man! I can't stand the heat!"*

I was undeterred by the drought or the temperature. I had just one minor remaining problem, however—how to finance the trip. I had contributed all my meager savings toward the first year of college, and had none left. My parents were expecting me to work during the summer, to contribute toward the coming year. I readily acknowledged the fairness of that expectation. However, to me, this was a once-in-a-lifetime opportunity, or at least one that would be hard to duplicate, to be able to live with a Chinese family in Hong Kong and experience everyday life there first-hand. My proposal was to borrow the funds from my parents to make the trip; I figured I could eventually pay it back, and it would be well worth it.

My father was not easily persuaded. Finally I announced that if he wouldn't lend me the funds to go, I would borrow them elsewhere. He asked me where. I didn't really have a plan, but one of my good friends, Toshi Moriguchi, whose family owned what was then a small mom-and-pop grocery store called Uwajimaya, liked to play pool and always seemed to have a wad of bills in his pocket. "From Toshi," I said. My father finally said that if I was determined to borrow the funds and go, he would lend me the money. Fortunately the rent would be free. We agreed on the sum of $750, which would include both airfare and a little spending money while I was there.

I wrote Bruce immediately to let him know that I would be arriving on June 26. When I later told him about the last-minute negotiations to secure the necessary funds, he was very amused at what he thought was a rather strange family relationship—the concept of a parent lending funds to his son for something like that, as well as the idea of conducting such a negotiation over the loan. He told me that in a Chinese family, the parents would either provide the funds to the son, as a gift, or else the son would not go.

Bruce responded immediately with another aerogramme to confirm, and with some final advice:

"I'm very happy to hear that you'll come on the 26th. . .You are very welcome in my house. The temperature is hot and man believe me it's hot. You've better ready to bring some thin clothings [sic]. By the way, remember that Hong Kong is like this—they respect your clothing first before they respect you! Remember to dress sharp. Of course, it's all right to dress like a slob once in a while. I do that too. Anyway, it will be a new experience and you'll dig it."

Doug, I'm very happy to hear that you'll come on the 26th, however, do write again and let me know the definite date, hour of arrival, flight number, etc. I'm sure you'll know. You are very welcome in my house.

The temperature is hot and man believe me it's hot. You'd better ready ~~some~~ to bring some thin clothings. By the way, remember this Hong Kong is like this ___ they respect your clothing first before they respect you! Remember to dress sharp. Of course, it's all right to dress like a slob once in a while. I do this too.

Anyway, it will be a new experience and you'll dig it.

So write and let me know all the information by the way, in your next letter, let me know of the situation down in the S.F. Club.

Bruce

Bruce knew whom he was talking to. I packed with the sharpest clothes I had (which isn't saying much), and boarded the plane to Hong Kong with tremendous excitement and anticipation. Except for a couple of trips to Canada—a camping trip to Vancouver Island and the demonstration with Bruce in Vancouver, B.C.'s Chinatown—this would be my first journey outside of the United States.

At the time, I didn't think much about why Bruce invited me. We were friends—why wouldn't he? In later years, especially when someone writing an article on Bruce would ask me that question, I thought more about it. And realized I didn't have any better an answer. Forty years later, a book by Bruce's brothers and sisters was published, and I read with interest about my visit from their point of view.

According to Robert and Phoebe, the brother and sister that were living at home then: "It's important to mention that having Doug stay with us was a very big move on Bruce's part. Bruce would have never brought home anyone whom he felt was undeserving or disrespectful. He really liked Doug and wanted to share with him the Chinese culture. Bruce was smart and knew that Doug would appreciate the different world that [lay] ahead for him in Hong Kong."[65]

Bruce was right. That summer in Hong Kong is engraved in my memory.

ENDNOTES

59 Lee and Campbell, *The Dragon and the Tiger*, vol. 1, p. 250.

60 When Allen Joe first set eyes on the young, well-dressed Bruce, he thought he looked like a fashion model. Russo, *Striking Distance*, p. 78. Bruce's glasses also added to the overall impression, and even after extensive back-and-forth discussion of the martial arts, Joe had reservations about the youngster's skills in a real-world street fight, until he actually saw Bruce move. Lee and Campbell, *The Dragon and the Tiger*, vol. 1, p. 239.

61 This was probably the time when he initially drove in the wrong direction for a while when leaving Oakland. According to Linda, he drove a "hundred miles" before realizing he was headed the wrong way.

62 See Polly, *A Life*, pp. 147 and 226. The origin of the one-inch punch deserves a side note. Jim DeMile has claimed that he helped Bruce develop the one-inch punch, after which Bruce swore him to keep it a secret between them, even from Jesse Glover. Bax, *Disciples*, interview with Jim DeMile, p. 120. Jesse, on the other hand, reports that Bruce demonstrated the punch to him early on. Bax, *Number One*, p. 95. My suspicion is that if Jim did help Bruce develop the punch, the extent of the help is greatly exaggerated. When I asked LeRoy about this recently, he just smiled and alluded to the fact that Jim was a "self-promoter."

63 Some accounts imply that his trip back was just for two or three months during the "summer." E.g., see Polly, *A Life*, p. 116. But in one of his daytimers he records March 26, 1963 as the day he left Seattle for Hong Kong. I also have a distinct memory of it being in March, and in *Lee Siu Loong: Memories of the Dragon*, authored by his siblings and compiled by David Tadman, p. 20, there is a photo of Bruce with his parents and a family friend signed on the back by each and dated April 4, 1963. Bruce's brother Robert told me he didn't recall the exact date Bruce arrived back in Hong Kong, but confirmed that the date on the photo was accurate.

64 Or so I was told then. Years later, Lanston told me that the reason he wasn't able to go was because his mother didn't like Bruce. Lanston's mother had a heart of gold, but she was as formidable as Ruby Chow and thought Bruce was a smart alec who didn't show enough respect. Jacquie Kay, however, says it was indeed because of the seizures.

65 *Lee Siu Loong: Memories of the Dragon*, p. 70.

CHAPTER 7

A Dream Comes True

N 1963 PLANES did not fly directly from the mainland U.S. to Hong Kong. I stopped in Honolulu on the way and spent a couple of days with a friend from Yale, a Chinese-American kid whose family owned a motel a few blocks from Waikiki. Waikiki was then fairly relaxed, before all the high-rise hotels and other development along the beach.

On the last leg of the flight, from Honolulu, I met an attractive Eurasian girl from Hong Kong who had spent a year as an exchange student in the States. She later invited me to a dance party at her parents' country club. As I found out, it turned out to be part of a whole different world than the one Bruce had grown up in. The contrast was striking, and instructional. But that came later. When the plane finally arrived in Hong Kong, I was immediately introduced to Bruce's world. It was a dream come true. The gritty reality did nothing to dampen my enthusiasm.

At that time, Hong Kong was still a British colony. It had recently suffered a mass influx of refugees from China, and housing was at a premium. Shanty-towns had sprung up, families built shelters on the roofs of buildings and people slept in parks and on the street. Beggars were everywhere. The city was also experiencing a severe drought, and apartments were only able to run water for several hours every few days. Those less fortunate had to wait with their buckets in lines that could stretch for blocks.

Hong Kong then consisted of three parts. Most of the population of some three million or so lived either on the northern shore of Hong Kong Island or on Kowloon Peninsula, which faced the island across a harbor. These were the parts of Hong Kong that were ceded to the British in 1842 and 1860 by the Qing Dynasty in the aftermath of the Opium Wars. The third part of the colony, the rest of Kowloon and the New Territories, along with a number of other islands scattered around Hong Kong Island, was taken over by the British a few decades later under a 99-year lease, set to expire in 1997.

Hong Kong's airport then, Kai Tak, seemed like a small field cleared out of the middle of the tenements of Kowloon, with a runway sticking out into the harbor. When the plane came in for a landing, you felt that if you could open the plane's window, you could reach out and grab the laundry hanging from the windows and tiny verandas of the tenements across the street from the airport.

My immediate impression when I emerged from the plane and stepped down the gangway to the tarmac was the heat and humidity, and the heavy overpowering olfactory assault of the muggy air. The sweltering heat was debilitating, like stepping into a giant sauna. The thick tropical salt air was infused with the smell of rotting garbage and night soil and diesel fuel and scores of other smells I couldn't identify. By the time I picked out Bruce and several members of his family, patiently waiting in the arrivals area to greet me, I had already grown accustomed to the odor; but the muggy air drenched my entire body with beads of sweat all summer long. As I found out, air conditioning was not at all common.

Few people in Hong Kong then owned cars, and Bruce's family was no exception.[66] We all piled into a taxi for the ride from the airport to the Lee family's apartment. The ride was a short one, but exhilarating.

The taxi wove through narrow streets of pushcarts and lorries and double-deck buses, between tall narrow tenements and office buildings with crowded shops at street level, and colorful signs in Chinese characters that stuck out from the buildings, fighting for space over the sidewalks. Swarms of people filled the sidewalks, sitting in front of shops, standing at food stalls, coolies in undershirts and old ladies in black pajama-like pantsuits rubbing shoulders with businessmen in Western suits.

Bruce filled me in as we drove to the apartment, while I tried to assimilate the total stimulation of all of my senses.

———

THE LEE FAMILY lived on Nathan Road, a main thoroughfare that ran down the middle of Kowloon peninsula right to its tip in Tsimshatsui, where it met the road running along the waterfront past the Peninsula Hotel to the Star Ferry. They lived in an apartment building of several stories above some shops, a good ten- or fifteen-minute walk from the end of Nathan Road, past what were then the Gurkha barracks, across the street from a small hotel called the Shamrock Hotel.

The open entrance to the apartments above was between two shops. A stairway led up from the sidewalk to a small landing where a homeless man laid out his pallet every night—if we came home late in the evening we had to be careful stepping over him in the dark. Above that the stairs continued on up to a larger landing on the second floor where the Lees' apartment and one other was located. Two doors guarded the apartment: an outer one of thick bars, like a jail door, and a stout inner one with a peephole.

The apartment itself was anything but ostentatious; it over-flowed with the large household that lived there. The floors were made of dark solid wood. The walls were mostly dark wood or plaster with dark trim.

Inside the front door was a foyer with carved wooden Chinese furniture. To the left was a small kitchen and a couple of small back rooms where two of the women slept. On the right the foyer led into two larger rooms that opened to balconies overlooking Nathan Road.

The furthest room was used mainly as a bedroom, with two double bunks and dressers. Clothes hangers hung from the beds and furniture. A cupboard along one wall with glass doors contained a bunch of knickknacks. On the inner end of that room, away from the street, was the bathroom. As a result of the drought, which limited water to several hours every few days, the bathtub was used as a makeshift reservoir, along with every available bucket and spare pot. The water was rationed for essential purposes—cooking and washing and flushing the toilet.

On the opposite end of the bedroom was a narrow balcony that overhung the sidewalk below and was partially open to the outside. A temporary "bath" area had been curtained off at one end, and a chicken in a cage lived on the other with numerous potted plants in between. The bath area was the size of a small shower, just wide enough to stand up in, and was used to wash off with a bucket of water and a sponge. Several tropical birds warbled in cages up above.

The nearer room tripled as a dining room, living room and sleeping area. A refrigerator stood against the near wall, a dining

Bruce and father working out, Hong Kong, summer 1963
Courtesy of David Tadman

table sat in the middle of the room. Bruce's bunk was on the far end, just inside the balcony. The balcony was completely enclosed and held two additional bunks, one used by Bruce's younger brother Robert, and one which was allocated to me. The bunks were just bed frames with hard mats on them, more like sleeping platforms. In the oppressive Hong Kong summer heat, no bedclothes were necessary.

Most activity took place around the dining table, where the household gathered not just for meals but to chat or play games, or to read. A fan was set up in one corner, which I sat in front of a lot. Bruce also set up an ironing board in the room when he ironed his pants or shirts. He was meticulous in his dress, and did not think the women in the house were able to properly iron his clothes.

Bruce and author practicing, Hong Kong, summer 1963
Courtesy of David Tadman

THE LEE HOUSEHOLD that summer consisted of Bruce, his father and mother, a sister Phoebe, his younger brother Robert, a cousin Frank, an aunt and a servant, in addition to the chicken and other animals. His two oldest siblings—Agnes and Peter—no longer lived at home. A number of other relatives and friends were often around. I later learned that Phoebe had been adopted, but at the time I thought she was a biological sister. She was certainly treated the same as the other children.

Of necessity, everyone lived in close quarters. Because of the heat and humidity, the men often walked around in their underwear. At night, I wore pajama bottoms and nothing else. Perhaps inevitably, the color of my nipples earned me a nickname: *Jiu Lin Dak*, or "Pig Teat Doug."

The drought did not make things any easier. To take a bath, one took a small bucket of water into the curtained-off corner of the balcony and sponged off. Not that it did much good, since I was drenched in sweat within minutes after finishing the sponge bath, but it made me feel a little bit better, at least for a short while.

Only Bruce and Robert spoke English beyond a few words. My Mandarin, which I had just finished an intensive year of at Yale, turned out to be virtually worthless. It was not widely spoken in Hong Kong then, and no one in the Lee household spoke it. So if Bruce or Robert were not around to translate, I had to make do with pantomime and the few Cantonese words I was trying to learn. At least the Chinese written characters were the same for Mandarin and Cantonese speakers, so I didn't feel totally lost. I could write out basic words, like my Chinese name, for Bruce's father.

Brother Robert, then fourteen, was a younger impish version of Bruce with equally excellent English. His nickname, *Gau-jai* ("Little Dog" or "Dog Boy"), seemed to fit him perfectly. There was also a friend of Robert who was always around, a skinny little kid with a crewcut and thick glasses, Gordon Tsoi (pronounced "Choy"), called *Tsoi-jai*, or "Little Tsoi." A cousin, Tony Lai, the same age as Robert, also spent a lot of time with them, sometimes sleeping over and sharing Robert's bunk along with Tsoi-jai.

Bruce's father, Lee Hoi Chuen, was a slight, kindly, generous, unpretentious man who was well known throughout Hong Kong as a former Cantonese opera star and film actor. He owned one Western suit which he wore if occasion demanded, but otherwise went around in loose-fitting Chinese clothes. I learned that in the past Bruce's father had smoked his share of opium, but he had given it up several years before and seemed fit and healthy. It must have taken its toll, however, since he died at age 64 less than two years after my stay. He practiced *t'ai chi* in a nearby park, which he had apparently taken up because of health concerns around the time he quit smoking opium.

Bruce's mother, Grace, was a warm, gracious woman. As mentioned earlier, she was part Caucasian, but her precise racial makeup is not entirely clear. That summer, I assumed from her appearance that she was mostly Chinese, with a smattering of European blood. Both Bruce and Robert looked predominantly Chinese to me. Of course appearances are at best a rough indication. My own two children, half-white and half-Japanese, show their Asian half to varying degrees. And our two granddaughters, each a quarter Asian, are even more disparate—one looks decidedly Asian, the other has red hair and could easily pass as Welsh or Irish. In the end, the details don't matter.

Bruce never dwelled on it, but I believe that his partial Caucasian ancestry influenced him in subtle ways. Perhaps the discrimination he faced from other Chinese because of his mixed heritage partially fueled his willingness to break with tradition. He was proud of being Chinese and of Chinese culture, but felt few compunctions in departing from what he called the "starched classicism" of some *gung fu* schools.

———

I LEARNED A number of things that summer, including the many ways that cultural differences could manifest. At my very first meal at the Lee table, the first course was a soup of clear broth and some vegetables. A large tureen was placed in the middle of the table and we were each ladled out a bowl. I trotted out my best manners. I sat up straight, making sure not to slouch and being careful not to slurp my soup, as my mother had taught me, bringing each spoonful to my mouth and sipping it with a minimum of sound.

After a minute or so Bruce leaned over to me and whispered in my ear: "Make a little noise." He told me later that it was polite at a Chinese meal to slurp your soup or noodles, to show your appreciation. Needless to say, my parents thought I was a real pain when I returned home at the end of the summer and made a point of telling them how slurping was not something that was universally frowned upon.

Bruce made constant efforts to educate me in the nuances of Chinese etiquette. But try as he might to anticipate the blunders of his *gwai lou* friend, he was up against an obtuseness that was hard to penetrate.

Shortly after I arrived I was asked if I wanted to change any money. I produced some of my stake and one of the family members went out to convert it at a nearby money-changer's stall. When he returned Bruce intercepted the wad of Hong Kong dollars that was handed over and made an elaborate show of counting it out in front of me slowly, not once, but twice. Then he handed it over to me, hoping I would just stick it in my pocket. But nothing clicked: I automatically counted it again before folding it away. Later Bruce told me that to openly count money that is handed you by someone you know implies distrust and is thus rude. Knowing that Americans often routinely counted money they received, he had tried to short-circuit that habit by openly counting it for me before he handed it over. To no avail.

All summer I struggled with subtleties of behavior and relation-ships that were often hard for me to sort out in real time. And where language was involved, the struggle was even harder. Sometimes, in my desire to use the Cantonese which I was starting to pick up, I managed to cause offense. One time we met a family friend on the street, a personable woman with a sense of humor whom I believe was married to someone in the film business. I had met her before, and she said something to me in a teasing way. My Cantonese was not adequate enough to banter back, and I said, "*Mo cho a!*" as a retort without thinking. The woman frowned slightly and I could tell that Bruce was not pleased. The phrase I had used literally meant "don't speak." But as I was later informed, it was the equivalent of "shut up"; and when used in the manner I had was considered quite rude, especially when spoken to a woman of her station.

In retrospect, Bruce was very patient when I messed up. One of the only other times he really got upset with me was when I over-reacted to a prank that his brother and Tsoi-jai pulled on me later in the summer.

———

SOMETIMES THE *faux pas* in Cantonese were ones I couldn't anticipate, even with greater forethought. Cantonese, like the other Chinese dialects, is a tonal language. Sounds which are otherwise identical or similar in pronunciation can have a radically different meaning with a different tone. After a year of intensive Mandarin my freshman year, I could speak it reasonably well. But Mandarin has only four basic tones. Cantonese has seven tones, and for me it was sometimes impossible to hear the differences between the tones, let alone remember them.

One night the Lee family and I sat around the table after dinner playing a simple board game. Each player had a marker that advanced around the board, and took turns throwing a die. Each face of the die had a picture of a different animal. I don't recall all the details of the game, but the first person to shout out the name of the animal showing on the upturned face of the die was able to advance his or her marker along the board's path some number of spaces, the object being to get to the end of the path before anyone else. I also don't recall all of the various animals on the six sides of the die, but one of them I remember very clearly—a crab.

The game became quite competitive. Each time the die was rolled all the players would jostle for the best view as it rolled to a stop and try to shout out the name of the correct animal before anyone else. I had had to learn the six animal names in Cantonese in order to play the game, which slowed my reaction slightly as I mentally translated the name of the animal into Cantonese. The word for "crab" was *haai*, pronounced with a lower tone. In the excitement of the game, however, my voice rose in pitch. Whenever the crab came up I would shout out *"hai!"* with a high even tone and shortened vowel sound. The women in the house, both the ones playing and the ones observing, seemed quite amused, and giggled whenever I yelled out my version of "crab." Finally Bruce took me aside and explained the difference in pronunciation between the word for "crab" and an earthy word for "vagina." After that, I was reluctant to yell out the word for crab whenever it came up, which was my excuse for subsequently losing the game.

BRUCE GOT A kick out of practical jokes. Not surprisingly, his younger brother Robert and his pals picked up that tendency.

Because of the drought, and the fact that the water stored in the bathtub and elsewhere was rationed, our baths were limited to every other day or so. Even though in the ever-present humidity I would be soaked with sweat soon after a bath, I looked forward to the brief respite when it was my turn. The screened-off corner of the balcony where the sponge-baths were taken was cramped, and I had barely enough room behind the full-length "shower" curtain to access the bucket of water on the floor if I bent my knees when I leaned over. One day when I was taking my bath, as I bent over

Bruce and author practicing on rooftop, Hong Kong, summer 1963
Courtesy of the Bruce Lee Family Archive

to replenish the sponge, I thought I felt something dust my skin. I thought it might be a moth or bug of some kind, but didn't think anything more of it, even when I felt it again. I also didn't think twice about the stool that was sitting just outside the curtain when I finished up. I dried myself and got partially dressed, then went back to my bunk to put on the rest of my clothes.

Robert and his pal Tsoi-jai were sitting on Robert's bunk. They seemed to be watching me expectantly, but I didn't think much about that, either. After a minute or so, though, I started to feel itchy and began to reach underneath my shirt to scratch. By then I was already sweaty again, and my damp shirt stuck to my body. Robert and Tsoi-jai were unable to contain themselves and began laughing. I asked what they were laughing at, and they asked me if I had felt anything when I was sponging off. I shrugged, still not understanding. Then they showed me a small can of something, which they told me was itching powder. Tsoi-jai had climbed on the stool to sprinkle it onto me over the top of the curtain while I was taking my sponge-bath.

I exploded and grabbed Tsoi-jai's upper arm, yanking him and giving him a toss. He was literally half my size—well under 100 pounds—and he went flying a little further than I intended. He wasn't hurt, but seemed a little shaken up by the burst of anger. Bruce was in the main room, laughing at the practical joke, but came to see what the commotion was all about.

He quickly became very displeased when he saw Tsoi-jai sprawled on Robert's bunk, rubbing his arm theatrically, and realized what had transpired. He let me know in no uncertain terms that it was not acceptable to act out against someone who was so much smaller, regardless of the provocation. Tsoi-jai played it up for all it was worth, but when I calmed down I felt somewhat bad, even though the itching powder was no fun and I didn't get to sponge off again. As I observed later, Bruce himself was beginning to put the restraint he was preaching into practice.

———

BRUCE'S OWN PRACTICAL jokes were more elaborate. The object of one of them was the Hong Kong police, which along with British soldiers constituted the two categories of beings he disliked the most. In the case of the police, he considered them to be corrupt and overbearing. Back then, the officers were mostly British and the street cops were mostly Chinese. Most of the Chinese police did not speak any English, but ones who sported a red bar on one of their sleeves were supposed to be able to. According to Bruce, however, even those spoke only rudimentary English.

Once we spotted a cop with a red bar, my job was to approach and ask him if he knew the way to the Canton Theater. In fact, there was a Canton Road nearby, but no Canton Theater. The policeman's brow would become furrowed and in broken English he would ask me if I wanted to go to Canton Road. No, I'd say, I was supposed to meet a friend at the Canton Theater. I would then launch into a long monologue about how I knew there was a Canton Road but that I was explicitly told to meet him at the Theater, not the Road. This was delivered as rapidly as I could, and verged on being double-talk. The cop would invariably become even more confused and simply repeat, "Canton Road?" Finally, after a few such back-and-forths, I was supposed to say to the cop, "*Lei ngi-ngi ngam-ngam jou matye?*", which loosely translated as, "What the hell are you mumbling about?" This was timed just as Bruce walked up to ask if he could help. I would turn to Bruce and tell him that I was trying to get directions to Canton Theater. He would reply that he was going that way and would show me. We would amble off together, leaving the cop standing there, wondering if he had somehow been made a fool of.

Bruce also took great delight in faking fights in front of Chinese onlookers. We practiced our routine: two roundhouse swings from me which he blocked with his forearms, then a stiff uppercut from him to my stomach which I had to make sure I tightened in time. Once we pulled this off as we got off the elevator at the ground floor of the high-rise apartment where Bruce's teacher Yip Man lived. We timed it so we emerged from the elevator arguing loudly, then swung into our skit in front of the people who were waiting for the elevator. Bruce thought it was amusing to stage a scene where a big foreigner got bested by a smaller Chinese guy.

These routines were typical of Bruce's sense of humor, which did not depend on the object of his practical joke ever knowing that there had been a joke of any kind. He once recounted an incident, before he left Hong Kong for the States, when he was taunted by a street tough. Instead of facing him as he normally would and dispatching him with straightforward punches and kicks, he affected a feminine swish and raised his hands in an ungainly defensive posture. When the tough swung, Bruce blocked the punch with an awkward jerk of his arm, then clumsily delivered a backhand flick to the man's groin, as if it were an accident. As his opponent doubled over in pain, Bruce put his hand over his mouth and tittered, then swished his hips as he walked away. When I asked him why he did that, Bruce laughed and said, "If a guy gets beaten by someone who's bigger or stronger than he is, he can accept that. But if he thinks he's been beaten by a fairy, he'll be pissed off for the rest of his life."

———

BRUCE ALSO LIKED telling jokes. They often verged on corny, and were sometimes risqué but never really raunchy. Some of his jokes made fun of stereotypes, either American stereotypes of Chinese, or vice versa. One of them depicted an American tourist in Hong Kong walking by a tailor's shop and seeing a suit he liked in the window. The tourist walked into the shop and brought the tailor outside to point at the suit, asking in an exaggerated pidgin, "Suit—how muchee?" Bruce would mimic the American's version of a Chinese accent as he repeated it several times to the stoic tailor, then drew himself erect to deliver the tailor's response. "Sir," Bruce would say in proper British English as he imitated the dignified manner of the tailor, "it would greatly facilitate our transaction if you would converse in your native language."

One of his favorite jokes made fun in the other direction—the joke recounted earlier about the American who ordered fried rice in a Chinese restaurant. I remember several other of Bruce's jokes, including one about a parrot in a pet store that had the magical property of disappearing any nearby object that was prefaced by someone saying the word "mungafunga." For instance, if someone said "mungafunga that chair," the chair would immediately disappear. In the joke, after verifying that the parrot indeed had such ability, a customer in the pet store bought the parrot and took it home to show his friends. When he explained to his first friend what the parrot could do, the punch line was the skeptical friend scoffing, "Mungafunga my ass!"

In still another joke, one that was mildly off-color, which I remember him telling in Cantonese to a female family friend in the movie business, the punch line was "buy a hair net." The friend seemed amused by the joke, but not as much as it amused Bruce to tell it.

I'm not sure why I can remember so many of Bruce's jokes. I think it's not the jokes themselves so much, but the hilarious way he would deliver them with such glee.

ENDNOTES

66 Brother Robert confirms that the family had a car and driver in the past, but I don't remember them having one in the summer of 1963. I believe by that time his father had simplified his life. Robert recalls that the driver, Ah Leung, had a bad memory and they would follow him around to try to find where he had parked the car, which upset his father.

Author with Eva Tso and Bruce, Hong Kong, summer 1963
Courtesy of David Tadman

CHAPTER 8
Baak Ma Dak in Hong Kong

BRUCE WAS THE perfect host that summer, taking a lot of time to show me the ropes and introduce me to people and to everyday Hong Kong life. Just a few blocks from Nathan Road, in Mong Kok, the streets at night were teeming with hawkers and food stands and crowds of people looking to buy something or have a meal or just take in the scene. I especially remember the cages of snakes which the vendors peeled for their customers on the spot.

Usually it was Bruce and his cousin Frank, who was a few years older, who would show me the night life on the street. Robert was considered too young to go out; Bruce definitely played the role of a strict older brother and felt that Robert should not be out on the streets fighting and getting into trouble the way he used to do.

There were plenty of things to do. We ate out often, mostly Chinese but Bruce was also fond of a particular Russian restaurant we frequented a few times. Other favorites were light meals such as Shanghai fried rice or oyster sauce beef and rice.

He also enjoyed going to a bath house, at least once a week, where we would soak in a pool of hot water and then have a vigorous massage. With only sponge baths available at home due to the water shortage, visiting the bath house was especially welcome. I confess to feeling somewhat uncomfortable, lying by the side of the pool naked while a Chinese *masseur* kneaded my muscles, but Bruce seemed perfectly at ease. He told me that there were other establishments where the massage was performed by women, who also offered "extra services," but he preferred massages given by men because their hands were stronger.

Bruce certainly seemed to enjoy the massages, and was greatly amused by my reaction to some of the more forceful techniques. I came to dread one technique in particular—one where the *masseur* dug in deep with his thumb and forefinger on either side of my Achilles tendon. I think the *masseur* went out of his way to dig in and then pluck it like a harp string, just to see me jump.

We also spent time doing more mundane things. One of the first things Bruce took me to do was to have some clothes made. I hadn't brought anything near what he considered sharp enough for going out, but clothing could be made cheaply then in Hong Kong, even considering the modest stash I had brought along. We visited a tailor used by the family who had a shop nearby, and I had a suit made out of a grayish, almost iridescent silk which I thought was quite the fashion statement, plus a few shirts. The suit cost about thirty U.S. dollars.

Bruce also had several suits made himself. He had specific ideas about the style of the lapels and side pockets, as well as the cut of the gorges and curve of the bottom corners where the two sides came together in the front, and drew pictures of what he wanted for the tailor. That may have been the first time I realized what a good artist Bruce was. He had an easy flowing hand that could

Bruce introducing author at wedding party, Hong Kong, summer 1963 *(left)*

Bruce and bother Robert goofing around at wedding party, Hong Kong, summer 1963 *(below)*

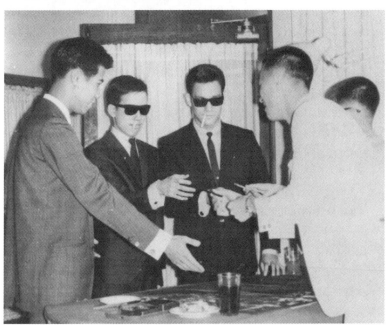

sketch whatever he visualized, as his later sketches of martial arts stances and moves showed.

Another excursion we made was to a carver who specialized in engraving names on seals (or chops), commonly used in China to sign documents or artwork with a red ink or cinnabar paste. I decided to have a seal made for myself and for each of my family members. I selected a blank stone seal for each one, cylinders or rectangular prisms which were already pieces of art in their own right, carved with animals or other designs. I didn't want the seals inscribed with Western lettering, so I had to select appropriate Chinese characters for each one.

In my case, it was easy—I used the three characters for the Chinese name that Bruce had given me (*Baak Ma Dak*), plus the character for "seal." My parents and brothers did not have Chinese names, however, so I decided to come up with an appropriate phrase for each one. Since my Cantonese was nowhere near adequate for the task, Bruce had to consult with the seal carver in each case to help me come up with the inscription. My youngest brother, Cam, was then nine but already had a small posse of friends that he led around. We finally settled on a Chinese expression that meant something like "little gang leader."

I recall that Bruce became rather upset with that selection when he had to communicate it to the carver. Apparently he thought it was not an appropriate inscription for a formal seal.

———

BRUCE ALSO INTRODUCED me to various people in the movie industry that he knew from his days as a child movie actor before he took off for the States. He had been in over twenty films, and his father in more. The family remained on good terms with a number of people in the industry. Bruce also introduced me to several starlets,

Dinner in Hong Kong with Bruce and Eva Tso et al., summer 1963

one of whom I developed a mild crush on. Unfortunately, none of them spoke English or Mandarin, and my Cantonese was not up to carrying on a meaningful conversation. But it was fun being included in get-togethers, such as once when we were invited to a young woman's apartment to practice the cha-cha.

The 1958 Hong Kong cha-cha champion had not forgotten his moves. As I found out, he had invented a number of unique steps which highlighted his grace as well as his humor. He taught several of the steps to both the young lady and me. I was impressed—and very envious—of the effortlessness with which he used his dancing skills to spend time with young women in a very natural and non-threatening way.

One acquaintance in particular from the movie circles went out of her way to include me in various functions and excursions, a kindly woman in her mid-forties named Eva Tso. Mrs. Tso was the wife of a well-known Cantonese movie star whom I was told had won an Asian film award for best actor the previous two years.

Author and Eunice
Lam, with Bruce
photo-bombing in
background, Hong Kong,
summer 1963. Eunice
later married Bruce's
brother Peter.
Courtesy of David Tadman

She took us just about everywhere there was to go in Hong Kong—
to the top of the Peak on Hong Kong side; out into the New territories to visit ancient villages with high walls and moats surrounded
by paddy fields and water buffaloes; and to small mountain-circled
inlets with fleets of fishing junks and sampans beached on the sandy
shores, and little children splashing nude in the gentle waves.

One time she invited us as guests on a cruise out into the islands
around Hong Kong. We swam and ended up at Aberdeen, on the far
side of Hong Kong Island, for dinner at a floating restaurant. The
cruise included a number of movie stars, and Bruce managed to
get us seated as the only two males at a table with about ten female
stars. But I couldn't speak to any of them, either.

***

EARLY IN THE summer, Bruce introduced me to a young lady who
spoke good English, named Shirley. She worked as a ground stew-
ardess for Cathay Pacific, and was a couple of years older than I.
Bruce had also dated her in the past, but she didn't seem to mind

either the age difference or that he was "passing her on." I quickly realized that dating in Hong Kong was entirely different from what I was used to back home.

First of all, no one I knew in Hong Kong had a car. And even if I had access to one, it wouldn't have made sense to use it. Traffic was terrible, parking was expensive and difficult, and there was nowhere to go at the end of an evening to park and "watch the submarine races." One exception to that may have been on the Hong Kong side, across the harbor, where there were more remote areas on the far side of the island away from the hustle and bustle of the densely populated districts between the shore and the steep hills that rose up from the water. But there was no easy way then to get over to Hong Kong side by car. This was long before car tunnels were dug connecting Kowloon and Hong Kong side; the main way to commute across between the two sides was a passenger ferry such as the Star Ferry.

So I had to use a taxi to pick up my date and squire her around. Since none of the taxi drivers then spoke any English (or Mandarin), I had to learn how to give directions in Cantonese. Although Shirley could of course give directions to the driver, I had to get to her apartment and then home again at the end of the evening. The first addresses I learned were hers and the Lee family's. I used both many times during the summer, and to this day I can rattle off both addresses in Cantonese. Hers was "*Lai Ji Gok Dou, Baat-sap-yat Hou*"—No. 81 Lai Chi Kok Road. The best way to give directions to get back to the Lee family's apartment was "*Lei Dun Dou, San Lak Jau Dim, doi min*"—"Nathan Road, right across from the Shamrock Hotel."

The second thing was to figure out somewhere to go—and to make sure I had a reservation. Even for the movies, Hong Kong then was so crowded that it was necessary to buy tickets in advance for specific seats for a specific showing. Needless to say, for a date I wanted a seat toward the back of the theater, preferably in the balcony.

Among other things, Bruce gave me tips on how to conduct myself on dates at the movies where every seat was filled, including lessons on how to engage in discreet petting without drawing undue attention from others. During classes in Seattle, Bruce had sometimes joked about using the "eagle claw" technique on dates. But in reality he was more subtle.

He demonstrated an incremental technique, which started with putting an arm around the girl's shoulder, then moving the other arm across your chest to rest it on the girl's closest arm. The next step was to gradually work the fingers so they were inserted between her arm and her side, just below her armpit at chest level, as unobtrusively as possible, then eventually to move a single finger casually up to the side of her breast. And so on. Bruce had me practice the technique on his brother Robert, who had to sit next to me on my bunk while I followed the step-by-step formula. I had no problem using the technique on Robert, but unfortunately was never very good at executing it in field conditions.

Bruce apparently had a much higher success rate. According to him, one time he was having such a good time in the movie theater that a guy in the row in front of him kept turning around to watch. Bruce said that he was finally forced to give the guy a stiff pop in the nose to get him to turn his attention back to the movie.

―――――

I WAS ALSO invited out for a party by the girl I met on the plane coming over to Hong Kong. She was half Chinese and half Canadian, and coincidentally had been an exchange student at the same high school in Lexington, Massachusetts that one of my freshman year roommates graduated from. She was quite attractive and of course spoke fluent English, as well as two dialects of Chinese, so I was anxious to accept the invitation. She lived on Hong Kong side, on the Peaks, which meant that her family was quite well-off; the party was at an exclusive country club.

To get there, I had to walk to the Star Ferry and take it across the harbor, then take a cab to the club. When Bruce's family heard where I was going for the evening, for which I sported my new silk suit, they gave the impression that they thought I was going off to Mars. At that time only a few of the wealthier Chinese associated with the British community at the private country clubs. Bruce's family, although certainly comfortable and well-connected in the Chinese community, did not travel in those circles. The evening was enjoyable, and interesting for the contrast it afforded, but I was thoroughly ensconced in Bruce's world.

We never double-dated in Hong Kong. I guess it was not a big thing, especially without a car. But we certainly talked about women. During one discussion he mentioned that Chinese women, especially those from well-to-do families, could be high mainte-nance. He seemed to be of the opinion that a non-Chinese wife might be a better option, although that didn't stop him from going out on plenty of dates. He didn't usually supply many details, but one time after he returned home from an excursion he told us about a minor altercation he had run into on the way home.

He had spent the evening on Hong Kong side (albeit not at a country club) and took the ferry back. He was dressed very nattily for the date, in one of the suits he had designed himself. Apparently his attire had caught the attention of a couple of punks who sat behind him on the ferry. They made loud comments about him and his fancy clothes. Bruce ignored them, and when the ferry docked began walking back toward Nathan Road. They followed him from the ferry terminal and continued to taunt him. When he walked faster to get away from them they kept apace right behind him, taunting him even more: "What's the rush, you have to hurry home to mama?" Finally Bruce couldn't take it anymore, so he whirled around to face them. He kicked the closest guy in the shin with the point of his shoe. The punk immediately folded up and rolled on the sidewalk, holding his shin. When Bruce turned to the second guy he backed up quickly, holding up his hands to signal he was out of it. Bruce turned and walked the rest of the way home unmolested.

Cousin Frank listened to the story after Bruce returned, then shook his head and laughed. "If that happened a few years ago," he said, "Bruce would have beaten both of them to a pulp as soon as he got off the ferry."[67]

I recall one Chinese expression which Bruce sometimes quoted: "There are one hundred schools of *gung fu*, but the best one is running." I doubt that he ever ran from anything, but he apparently was showing a lot more restraint.

BRUCE DEMONSTRATED THAT he could keep his temper in check in other ways, too. One evening the family and friends had gathered to celebrate the wedding of a cousin. The family's second-floor apartment was crowded with people and extra tables set up for food. In the midst of this festive atmosphere I noticed that a growing number of family members had bunched up by the apartment entrance. The inner door was open and a conversation of some sort was being conducted through the outer door of bars. It looked like Bruce had taken charge, not his father or cousin Frank.

Finally Bruce came over to me and explained what was happening. Apparently some local toughs had observed the comings and goings and realized a celebration of some sort was underway. They had knocked on the front door and asked for some "lucky money." Bruce told me to go out and try to bluster—maybe a white face would back the guys off; maybe they would think I was a British cop.

By then the barred door was open, with heavy discussion continuing on the stairwell. I eased past the family members and stepped up to the leader. They were not teenage delinquents, but older rugged-looking men.

The leader wore a tank-top undershirt and shorts, and was husky and well-muscled, with a hard-bitten expressionless look. But I loomed over him, leaning into his space. "*Lei yiu matye?* What do you want?" I demanded, in as threatening a tone as I could muster.

The man looked up at me without blinking and responded matter-of-factly, not intimidated a bit. I had no idea what he had said in Cantonese, so I just repeated my question, in a louder voice, trying to crowd him more. "*Lei yiu matye?*" He stood his ground and responded again. Finally Bruce pushed his way through the other family members with a disgusted look on his face. He said something to the man and handed him a couple of Hong Kong dollars. The men left.

Back inside, I asked Bruce why he hadn't told the leader to take a hike, and thrown him down the stairs if he persisted in his demands. Bruce showed no physical concern about the toughs. He wasn't afraid of them personally—he used to brawl with street hoods as a teenager.

"No use," he said. "If I did that, one night—bam! There'd be a rock through the window. Better just to give him a few dollars." One Hong Kong dollar was worth a little more than 17 U.S. cents then, so Bruce had given them the equivalent of about 35 cents.

The experience made a lasting impression on me. I realized that there were other, and sometimes more effective, ways to

Author with brother Robert and friend Tsoi-jai, Hong Kong, summer 1963

solve a problem, even when physical force seemed like a good immediate solution.

―――――――

WHEN BRUCE HAD other things to do, I often hung out with his younger brother Robert and cousin Tony and Tsoi-jai. The three of them were inseparable, and knew their way around Hong Kong quite well. They took me sight-seeing and on various excursions, like up the peak tram on Hong Kong side, up to the top of the mountain overlooking the central business district and the harbor, with Kowloon and the New Territories beyond.

Once they took me to an amusement park that had rides as well as games where you could try your hand at winning a pack of cigarettes or some other prize. The games were the kind that used to be seen at county fairs in the U.S., which looked easier than they actually were because the house had an edge that was not apparent. I had once worked in a booth in an Illinois fair where the object was to throw a ball at three bottles stacked in a pyramid, one perched on top of the other two. I remember being surprised when the manager of the booth showed me that two of the bottles were much heavier than the third one, and that I needed to place the heavier two on the bottom. The ball looked like a baseball but was a bit lighter, so it took almost a direct hit with speed to knock over one of the heavier bottles; and since the two bottom bottles were set up with a little space between them, it was almost impossible to knock over all three bottles with one throw.

I assumed that the games at the Hong Kong amusement park were similarly rigged. After watching one of them, however, we quickly figured out that we might have our own edge. This was a game where a number of ceramic saucers or small plates were arrayed in a grid over a wire mesh. The plates were placed maybe five inches apart, maybe ten in each row, six rows or so deep. A narrow counter blocked off the area where the attendant manned the array, with several feet between the counter and the plates. The plates were at table height, with plywood surrounding the frame that supported the mesh and plates. The object was to flip a coin—one of your own—so that it stayed in one of the dishes. But after watching a number of people try their luck, it was obvious that no matter how the coin was tossed, whether with a high or a low arc, if it hit a plate it invariably bounced or slid off into the space between that plate and the next one, and disappeared through the mesh into the hidden area below.

Robert and Tsoi-jai realized that I was quite a bit taller than anyone else in the crowd, and could just reach the first row of plates if I leaned over the counter. So when the attendant had his back to us, I slipped through the crowd, reached over to place a coin in one of the dishes in the front row, then faded back into the crowd. The amusement park was quite popular, and the crowd around this particular game was several people deep. As soon as I had slipped back into the crowd, Robert and Tsoi-jai would yell out that they had flipped a coin into a dish and demand a prize. The attendant turned around and almost did a double-take when he saw a coin in the first row of dishes. It was virtually impossible to flip a coin so that it stayed in the first plate it hit. Once in a while someone was able to flip a coin so that it bounced from one dish and managed to land in another one behind it without bouncing out. That technique didn't work for the first row of dishes, however.

The attendant was suspicious and slow to hand over a pack of cigarettes. He scanned the crowd but couldn't figure out how Tsoi-jai had been able to do it. Eventually he turned around again to straighten out the plates and I slipped forward a second time to reach over the counter and place a coin. Robert and Tsoi-jai began yelling again to demand a prize. Tsoi-jai especially had quite a loud voice for a small guy and made quite a din. Everyone in the crowd outside the counter had seen what had happened and seemed very amused. The attendant was certain that something was fishy this time, and took an even longer time to pay Tsoi-jai off. After the third time, the attendant spotted me at the back of the crowd and saw that some of the onlookers were grinning and looking at me. He quickly removed the first row of plates and stacked them up at the back of the booth. The second row of plates was too far to reach, even for me, so our scam was over.

Robert and his friends also took me shopping when I needed to pick up some gifts to take home. At one shop in Tsimshatsoi, where there was a lot of tourist traffic, I found some bamboo plates decorated with Chinese scenes and calligraphy which I thought would be nice. I used Robert as an interpreter and asked how much it would be if I bought a bunch of plates. The shopkeeper said something, and Robert and his pals all laughed and responded. Later they told me that the shopkeeper had offered to give them a kickback on what I bought if they could keep the price high. He became rather flustered when they told him I was a friend of the family.

Occasionally, they tired of taking care of Bruce's *gwai lou* friend. When they did, they had no compunctions about teasing me unmercifully. The knee I tore freshman year was still bothering me, and on bad days my limp was quite pronounced. One time when they were put out they followed me home a half block behind me, imitating my limp with great exaggeration the whole way.

They also enjoyed imitating my Cantonese accent. One phrase I had learned was *"Lei seung mseung tiu mou?"*, meaning, "Would you like to dance?" The pronunciation of *"seung"* was especially hard for me, and they would all contort their faces to imitate my tortured pronunciation of that phrase, delivered to an imagined young lady.

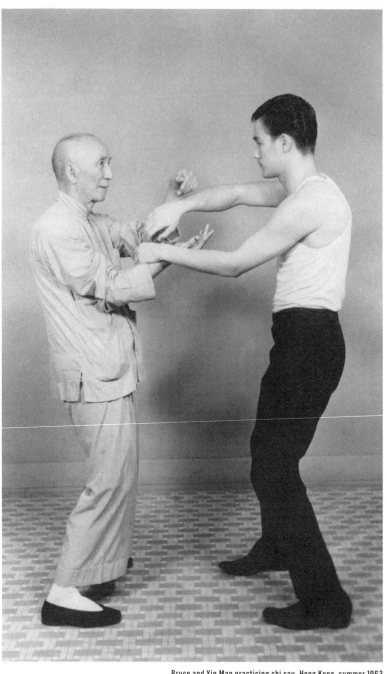

Bruce and Yip Man practicing chi sau, Hong Kong, summer 1963
Courtesy of the Bruce Lee Family Archive

But they helped me out a lot, and no doubt saved me from getting myself in trouble many times. They were great companions to whom I remain forever indebted. Along with the rest of the extended household, they made me feel at home and were an integral part of an experience which has stayed with me my whole life.

———————

BRUCE WORKED OUT periodically that summer with his Wing Chun teacher, Yip Man. Once or twice he took me to watch them work out after cautioning me to pretend that I didn't know any *gung fu*. Although in the States he was teaching anyone who was interested regardless of race, he was well aware that it was still a taboo to teach *gung fu* to non-Chinese, not only in Hong Kong but anywhere else. Out of respect for his teacher, he did not want to flout the fact that he had started teaching to non-Chinese.

Yip Man has since become well known as Bruce's teacher, and martial arts movies have been made in Hong Kong featuring him as the main character. But at that time he was not particularly known outside of Chinese martial arts circles in Hong Kong. He lived in an apartment near the top of a high-rise on Kowloon side, and used one of the rooms as a work-out area. He was a slight, unassuming man with a smile and a twinkle in his eye, an almost bald pate with a barely visible fuzz of gray hair on the sides. He was almost 70 then but still fit and powerful. No one else was present. After Bruce introduced me as a friend who was visiting from the U.S., they practiced *chi sau* ("sticking hands") in their undershirts while I sat and watched.

Bruce was younger and presumably stronger, and after one session I rashly asked Bruce whether he could take his teacher. As soon as the question popped out of my mouth I felt bad about asking it, but Bruce didn't react as if it were impertinent. He just deflected the question, and said something to the effect that Yip Man was getting on in years. I took it that Bruce considered his own physical abilities to be greater at that point, but was too polite to say so directly. And he clearly still thought that Yip Man had things to teach him.[68]

I didn't meet any of Yip Man's other students. I have since read that at some point before Bruce left Hong Kong for the States other students protested Bruce's inclusion in the class, after which Yip Man began teaching Bruce privately. Bruce never mentioned that to me, but it was probably just fine with him. Clearly he preferred one-on-one training to being part of a class.

I have also read that after he returned from his 1963 trip back to Hong Kong, he was so frustrated over his lack of progress when he worked out with some of the senior Wing Chun students, he thought of quitting *gung fu*.[69] I never saw any indication of anything like that. Nor did his wife, Linda. He apparently told Jesse that whereas he was the sixth best in Wing Chun when he left Hong Kong in 1959, when he returned in 1963 there were only three people he was unable to get by using *chi sau*—Yip Man, his assistant and one senior student.[70] That would certainly provide an impetus for him to continue developing methods to overcome an advanced *chi sau* practitioner, but hardly grounds to consider giving up *gung fu*.[71]

———

I HAD SEVERAL medical encounters in Hong Kong. The first two instances involved Western medicine, with mixed results. The third exposure involved traditional Chinese medicine, for which I am forever grateful.

I still had my teenage pimples, and one day Bruce handed me a tube of ointment he suggested I try. Unfortunately, it didn't do much to counteract the eruptions.

Later in the summer I developed a bad sore throat. Bruce's mother took me to a doctor who practiced Western medicine who diagnosed me as having tonsillitis. He gave me a penicillin shot and some medicine to take home, with a better result than the zit ointment. The total cost for doctor, shot and medicine came to about U.S. $3.

My ruined knee also continued to bother me. By the time I arrived in Hong Kong it had been over six months and still didn't seem to be getting any better, so I was resigned to having an operation after I returned to school in the fall to remove the torn meniscal cartilage. At some point during the summer Bruce's father mentioned a doctor they knew who practiced Chinese herbal medicine. He was known as being especially good with joint problems and broken bones. My budget hadn't taken that into account, but like everything else in Hong Kong the cost of the Chinese medicine was cheap, so I figured I had nothing to lose. I told Bruce's father that I would like to try it.

A day or so later the Chinese doctor showed up, and every morning after that. He was a short stocky man wearing short pants, with a cheerful smile and a gold tooth. He brought his own equipment, which included a small charcoal brazier as well as his bag of medicines. I took a seat in the foyer while he prepared a poultice of various herbs that looked like a mudpack, and heated it up on the brazier. He squatted while he waited for it to heat up, grinning and wiping the sweat off his brow with a handkerchief. It gave off a distinct medicinal aroma as it heated up.

When the poultice was smoking hot he applied it to my knee and held it there firmly as I writhed in pain. I protested in my rudimentary Cantonese, "*Hou yit! Hou yit!* Very hot!" But his grin just got wider. After a while the poultice cooled off and he would heat it up again. He repeated this procedure several times over the course of a half hour or so, then rubbed a pungent oil on my knee and massaged it into the skin.

After a couple of weeks a rash of large red pimples covered my knee. The doctor nodded approvingly. This, he explained, was the *fung*—the "wind"—coming out. I had no idea what that meant, but I didn't care. My knee was definitely getting better.

The original plan was to have the doctor come every day for three weeks, at a total cost of about U.S. $40. I thought that was reasonable, and if necessary was prepared to cover it out of the $100 I had set aside for the trip home. I also wrote my father and let him know about the treatments, and asked him to advance me an additional $40 to replenish my stash. He responded with a measure of skepticism and asked if I had "gone around the bend." But he sent me the $40.

By the end of the third week my knee was markedly better, and I could even use that leg to execute snapping *gung fu* kicks again—something I hadn't been able to do since I tore it. However, it wasn't completely healed. Because of Bruce's own medical needs, we had delayed our scheduled departure date a couple of times, so I had more time to continue the treatments if I wanted. I had used up the extra $40 sent by my father, and again debated whether to dip into the funds I had allocated for the return trip.

Bruce's father listened to Bruce and me discuss the problem one night around the dinner table. Finally he said something and Bruce turned to me. "He asked if the treatments were doing any good." I said they were. His father spoke some more. Bruce nodded and turned to me again. "He says if it's helping you, he'll pay for it."

I was overwhelmed by the gesture. I also felt bad imposing on his generosity, but in the end accepted. As it turned out, I was glad I did and profoundly in his debt. With the additional week or two of treatment my knee was as good as new. I have never had a problem with it since, whether back-country skiing or practicing *gung fu*.

When I returned to Seattle and told my family doctor, a crusty old German and old family friend, he scoffed. "Nonsense," he said.

According to him, there was no known substance that could be applied to the outside of the skin and cure that kind of an internal injury. "If there was anything to it, don't you think Western medicine would have heard of it after all these years?" It worked, I insisted. "Pure coincidence," he said. But it did work, as did the acupuncture I had years later for a different problem.

———————

BRUCE'S OWN MEDICAL experience toward the end of our stay in Hong Kong was of a different sort, and self-inflicted. For some reason, he decided to get circumcised. When I asked him why, he said it was his father's idea. But he never gave a good explanation of why his father thought it made sense, and I didn't press him. Maybe it was something he thought the girls in the States preferred.[72]

Bruce returned from the hospital with a halting, bow-legged walk, and immediately changed from the stylish tight pants he usually wore to a pair of loose-fitting Chinese pants he borrowed from his father. It was obvious that the operation was a more major one than he had anticipated. As I wrote home in an aerogramme, he walked around for a couple of weeks "like a mule [had] kicked him in the crotch."

As soon as he returned and changed his pants, all the males in the household crowded around to inspect the surgeon's handiwork. Bruce gingerly displayed his swollen purplish member in his hands to a symphony of sympathetic exclamations. It was quite a dramatic sight. I am sure he had second thoughts about the operation, and that if anyone else in the house had even been thinking about it, they changed their mind. Every morning after that until Bruce and I left for the States, we gathered around in a circle to inspect the progress from the day before. Bruce would produce his swollen member and the rest of us would commiserate.

As it turned out, the healing process took longer than antici-pated. Once Bruce went out wearing his own tight pants, but he returned to the apartment quickly and changed back to his father's loose-fitting pair. It was just too painful.

We had originally planned to return to the States, via Tokyo and Honolulu, on July 26. In anticipation of the operation, we changed the departure date to August 9. As that date approached, we decided to postpone our departure again. I was having such a great time that I joked to my father in an aerogramme that I might ask Yale for a year's leave of absence. I suggested to Bruce that we should push the date back even further, but he was reluctant to delay any longer. He had put Taky in charge of the class, but Taky was scheduled to leave on a trip back east sometime in the middle of the month, and Bruce wanted to get back. By the time we finally left, on August 15, Bruce had recovered sufficiently to resume his usual wardrobe.

ENDNOTES

67 My memory of the incident entails no mention of Bruce's companion being with him at the time the encounter occurred. Eunice Lam, who later married Bruce's brother Peter, apparently claims to have witnessed the encounter. See Polly, *A Life*, p. 119. My strong impression when Bruce told me the story was that he was returning home alone at that point of the evening, but perhaps Bruce elided her presence in his rendition.

68 I am quoted as having said that that was the first time I had ever seen Bruce "unable to dominate someone." Polly, *A Life*, p. 121, citing my interview in Paul Bax's *Disciples*. It is true that Bruce did not dominate during the workout. And Bruce apparently told Jesse Glover that he could still not get in on Yip Man while practicing *chi sau* during the 1963 trip; and that it was not until a later trip back to Hong Kong that he felt he prob-ably could. Glover, *Bruce Lee*, pp. 52-53. But *chi sau* is a training exercise, not an unfettered bout of sparring.

69 Polly, *A Life*, p. 118, citing Jim DeMile and Howard Williams.

70 Glover, *Bruce Lee*, p. 52.

71 According to Jim DeMile, the 1963 trip was when Bruce realized that he would never be able to best the senior students using *chi sau* and other Wing Chun techniques, since they were continuing to practice too, and that he needed to broaden his conceptual approach. Bax, *Disciples*, interview with Jim DeMile, p. 117.

72 In *Bruce Lee: A Life*, in notes to p. 121 on p. 527, Matthew Polly points to brother Robert's state-ment that the decision was Bruce's. He suggests that since I didn't speak Cantonese, I might have misunderstood. But Bruce told me in English that it was his father's idea. Still, it didn't add up to me that his father would want him to be circumcised. To my knowledge, none of the other males in the household had been, nor were they planning to be. Perhaps Bruce told me it was his father's idea because he figured I would think it odd for him to suddenly get circumcised at his age.

CHAPTER 9
On His Own

O N OUR WAY back, we stopped in Tokyo for a few days. Neither of us spoke any Japanese, but since it was on the way Bruce figured we may as well stop and take a look. We took the train into town from Haneda Airport (the monorail didn't open until a year later) and stayed at a businessman's hotel in the Marunouchi area of Tokyo, within walking distance of the Ginza.

Bruce was able to walk around by then, so we did some exploring. The first evening we stopped at a restaurant on the edge of Ginza. The waitresses didn't speak any English, but many restaurants in Japan have plastic models of their main dishes in the window, so we were able to point to what we wanted. After the meal we left a tip, which was common in Hong Kong as well as the States.

When we were a half block from the restaurant we heard a commotion behind us and turned around. Our waitress was running after us and yelling. Since she was wearing a *kimono* and *zōri* (flipflop-like sandals), she couldn't run very fast. We stopped and waited for her to catch up.

After she caught her breath she bowed and thrust her hand out, with all the money we had left for the tip. She said something in Japanese; we assumed she was telling us that we had forgotten something. We told her that it was meant as a tip, and repeated "Tip!" in a loud voice several times. We also pointed to the money and then to her, trying to pantomime that it was meant for her. But it didn't get through. So we eventually retrieved the money and returned her bow. Once we had the money back in our pockets, she handed us each a box of matches with her restaurant's name and logo on it, then bowed again. We realized that the customs were somewhat different in Japan than we were used to.

Back in the hotel Bruce suggested we get a massage, so we called the front desk. Two middle-aged ladies arrived and gave us vigorous massages as we lay side by side on our narrow twin beds in the tiny hotel room we shared. Neither of them spoke any English.

My only other memory from Tokyo is a couple of American GIs we ran into somewhere. The conversation at some point drifted to the martial arts, and I may have mentioned that Asian martial arts were more effective in a real fight than Western boxing because they were less constrained in their use of various techniques. One of the GIs had definite views about "fighting fair," and asserted that if someone ever kicked him in the balls during a fight he would take his revenge. Bruce remained mostly silent during this exchange. I was mildly surprised that he didn't demonstrate some of his moves to the guys in his inimitable way, but he was apparently still not fully recovered from his operation.

———

BY THE TIME we reached Honolulu, Bruce was pretty much back to par. We stayed in a cheap hotel near Waikiki. Ed Parker, a karate man who taught Elvis Presley, was in Honolulu for some reason. He

Bruce and author in Honolulu, summer 1963, with Ed Parker and group
(Ed is behind and immediately to the right of Bruce)
Courtesy of the Bruce Lee Family Archive

came over to our room and he and Bruce talked about the martial arts, with Bruce demonstrating some of his *gung fu*.[73]

A year later, after Bruce had moved down to Oakland, Ed arranged for him to demonstrate his "one-inch punch" at Ed's martial arts tournament in Long Beach. It was that demonstration, which some movie people saw, which has been credited as opening the door for Bruce's later run at Hollywood.

Bruce was also asked to give a demonstration to a *gung fu* school in Honolulu. He took me along to assist. There were fifty or so students and some instructors, all Chinese. I was mainly along to act as the dummy for Bruce's demo, but it was apparent from the way I stood and reacted that I knew some *gung fu*.

Afterwards one of the instructors came over to me. He was in his thirties or forties and had a cigarette dangling from his mouth. He asked if Bruce was teaching me, and I realized that what he meant was, did Bruce teach to non-Chinese. I had been told by a Chinese classmate at Yale who was from Hawaii that only Chinese took *gung fu* there, and karate was mostly for Japanese. But not until the instructor asked me point blank after the demo did it sink in. I told him that Bruce taught anyone who was sincerely interested—"even Chinese."

Meanwhile a number of students had surrounded Bruce with additional questions, and the same instructor approached the group. He asked Bruce how he would block a straight kick. Bruce offered to demonstrate. The man delivered a straight kick to the groin which Bruce blocked with a slap of his left hand to the top of the foot. After the block, Bruce spread his hands to indicate that that was the way it was done as he explained the block. But the man hadn't withdrawn his foot all the way to the ground. He left it half-extended in the air, and as Bruce spread his hands the man gave his foot a little flick. "See," he said. "You were open there."

Bruce was smoldering, but didn't respond directly. He continued explaining various techniques and offered to demonstrate a different block. The man obliged and threw a punch, but this time Bruce did not withdraw after blocking it. He trapped the punch and threw a counter of his own, slow enough so that the man could easily block it with his free hand. As soon as he did, Bruce grabbed the hand and drew it down with a *laap sau* ("pulling hand"), effectively pinning both arms. The force and speed of the second pull was so great that the man's whole body jerked and the cigarette went flying out of his mouth. Bruce calmly continued his exposition for a while with the man's arms still pinned, demonstrating various follow-up punches with his free hand. Each time he demonstrated a follow-up maneuver the man's whole body would jerk again. Finally, his revenge complete, he let the man go.

AFTER HAWAII, WE stopped in Oakland to see James Lee, who was then 43 years old. He taught and worked out in his two-car garage, which he had converted into a gym and workout area with his own special training equipment.

To me, James sounded like he had a Brooklyn accent. He seemed surprised when I asked him if he had grown up in Brooklyn; he had lived his whole life in the Bay Area. Bruce and James shared a practical approach to the martial arts, and seemed to get along very well.

They also shared another characteristic—the willingness to pass their knowledge on to non-Chinese. James invited one of his students over to the house when we were there—Al Novak. Al was a World War II veteran who had seen a lot of action,[74] a huge man at nearly 300 pounds, most of it muscle. When Bruce demonstrated *chi sau* with Al, I was impressed that he moved Al around like any other opponent, notwithstanding his size. In *chi sau*, as then practiced by Bruce, one must exert a constant outward force with the arms when they come in contact with the opponent. If the opponent is strong, the arms can tire very quickly. But Al's size didn't seem to present any problem for him.

Al's arms were covered with tattoos, which made him seem even more physically imposing. I don't recall the context, but at one point I made the remark that he must be able to take 95% of the population. Al demurred, saying that there were a lot of tough guys out there. I thought he was being modest, but he seemed sincere. Neither Bruce nor James disagreed. It got me to thinking that maybe there were a lot of things in the world that I hadn't yet run across.

Class in University District, Seattle, fall 1963

WHEN WE GOT back to Seattle I plunged back into the *gung fu* class for the few weeks before it was time to take off for college. By then the class had moved to a storefront in the University District. I saw that the classes were a bit more formal, with Bruce and the assistant instructors wearing uniforms and the students wearing a skimpy vest over their T-shirts. The vest had a logo designed by Bruce for the Jun Fan Gung Fu Institute, consisting of a stylized yin/yang symbol with curved arrows on the sides. It wasn't much, but it was the first time I had seen students wearing anything in particular for class.

Bruce was still the same jokester. One of the students was an optometrist who supplied Bruce with his contact lenses. Bruce also had several tinted lenses made, including one that was a greyish color with red "veins" radiating from the pupil. Bruce delighted in turning his back to put them in, then turning back around with widened eyes to startle people with his seemingly bloodshot eyes.

Lanston was also in the class, and he hung around with Bruce and me after class was over. He spoke Toisan, a Cantonese dialect spoken by many Chinese in American Chinatowns then. Bruce teased him that it was a "country" dialect, not as sophisticated as the Hong Kong dialect which Bruce spoke.

Lanston was a feisty guy who sometimes found it hard to play second fiddle to Bruce, as a result of which Bruce sometimes became a little more physical with Lanston when we were sparring or horsing around. Not that Bruce ever hit him or really hurt him, but Bruce's forearms were as hard as rocks from his long workouts on his teakwood dummy, so his blocks could hurt almost as much as his punches.

Sometimes he picked Lanston up at his house or dropped him off, but Bruce didn't like to hang out there because he didn't get along with Lanston's mother. Although I hadn't known Lanston well in high school, my brother Mike and I developed a close friendship with him, and Mike hung around with him often while I was away at college.

Once he and Mike visited one of Lanston's family's Chinese restaurants in Eastern Washington. Lanston had a seizure while driving the car back across the Cascade Mountains over Snoqualmie Pass, in a snowstorm. The car veered off the road into a gully, but fortunately they sustained only minor injuries. In Mike's case, it was a scar on the forehead sustained when he hit the windshield.

ABOUT THE TIME I left to drive back east for my sophomore year, Bruce was getting ready to move out of Ruby Chow's. I had written to my parents from Hong Kong to ask if Bruce could stay with them until he found a new place, and they had agreed. His plan was to move into the new space he had rented in the University District for the class, which had showers and a room in the back where he could stay, but it wasn't yet fixed up. My brother Mike had moved into my bedroom, which had two beds, and Bruce shared the room with him. Mike tells me that Bruce often kept him up late at night, telling corny jokes, then tittering underneath his covers after delivering the punch line.

Bruce stayed at my parents' for a month or so before moving into the University District space. My parents fed Bruce too, but American cooking was not to his taste and he often went down to Chinatown or over to Jacquie Kay's for dinner, explaining to my mother that he needed rice. I think my mother also did Bruce's laundry, but she was impressed that he got up every morning to iron his own clothes.

Class in University District, Seattle, fall 1963
Top: Sue Ann Kay and author in foreground; bottom: Lanston Chinn and Taky in foreground
Courtesy of David Tadman

Once when he was ironing his clothes in the morning my brothers were sitting at the breakfast table eating cereal. My youngest brother, Cam, let out a loud fart. Bruce looked at him with a smirk and said, "You must be tired."

Cam looked back at him with befuddlement. "What?"

"Your butt just snored," Bruce said.

Mike had just started his senior year in high school. He was a rugged kid, who boxed and played football for Garfield High, being selected as an All-City guard that year. Mike never took *gung fu*, but Bruce always enjoyed an audience and loved to demonstrate various moves.

One of the moves was a clavicle hold which Bruce used to immobilize someone, digging his fingers down behind the top of the clavicle. It was painful, but didn't cause any lasting injury. Mike asked once for a demonstration, and Bruce obliged. Once was enough. He also apparently sometimes used the maneuver on Lanston when Lanston popped off, causing him to "wriggle around like a frog."[75]

Once while joking around at night Mike suggested to Bruce that he could take a baseball bat to Bruce when he was sleeping. Bruce allowed as how he might be able to, but he'd better make sure the first blow landed.

———

SOMETIME IN THE early fall of 1963, Bruce met his wife to be, Linda Emery. She had seen him earlier in the year, during her senior year of high school, when he visited Garfield, but hadn't actually met him. As she started freshman year at the University of Washington, her friend Sue Ann Kay introduced her and she joined the *gung fu* class.

Also during the fall, in one of life's great ironies, Bruce flunked his draft physical due to an undescended testicle.[76] It's not clear why it mattered to the Army, but it obviously didn't hamper Bruce's fighting ability.

When I returned for Christmas break, I rejoined the class. By then Bruce and Linda were dating. There was only one problem, however—she was still living at home, and her parents did not approve of interracial dating. In high school she had briefly dated a Eurasian boy. I don't know how she managed it then, or at other times with Bruce, but on one occasion over Christmas break the problem was solved with a double date.

I had asked out a Chinese girl who had the same problem. As I recall, Bruce drove. We picked Linda up first, where she lived on Capitol Hill. I went up to the door and rang the bell and met her parents. Perhaps because I had been Garfield valedictorian the year before, and was then attending Yale, they seemed very congenial.

Next we drove to pick up my date on Beacon Hill. This time Bruce went to the door. As a polite young Chinese man who was attending the University of Washington, her parents were happy with Bruce. When they got back to the car, we switched.

I don't remember what we did for the evening—probably went to see a movie. But I do recall the end of the evening. When we dropped my date off and I saw her to the door, I was awarded with a good night kiss. It was a fairly chaste one, but Bruce later let me know that "proper" Chinese girls didn't kiss on the first date.[77]

ENDNOTES

73 It is unclear when James Lee first introduced Bruce to Ed Parker. It was probably during a trip of Bruce's down to Oakland in early 1963, before he left for his visit back to Hong Kong. My recollection is that when Ed came to our hotel room in August, they had already met. But it may be that James knew Bruce and Ed were going to be in Honolulu at the same time, and arranged for them to meet there.

74 Russo, *Striking Distance*, p. 86.

75 Youngest brother Cam claimed that Bruce used the clavicle hold on him if he gave Bruce too much lip. I have no doubt that Cam gave him lip, but I have my doubts that Bruce used the clavicle hold on him to any extent, since he was only nine at the time. Mike confirms that Bruce may have demonstrated it to our younger brothers, but never used it on them for discipline.

76 A November 4, 1963 notification from the Selective Service to "Jun Fon Lee AKA Bruce Lee" classified him as IV-F. From time to time, various reasons have been given as to why Bruce flunked the physical, but Bruce once told me matter-of-factly that it was due to an undescended testicle.

77 He may or may not have applied that stricture to him and Linda. Linda describes their first date, where he took her to dinner at the Space Needle, as closing with a light good-night kiss. Linda Lee, *The Bruce Lee Story*, p. 12. More recently, she said that they didn't kiss on their first date. When I pointed out the description in her book she laughed and said, "I guess it wasn't that memorable."

Bruce practicing on teakwood dummy
Courtesy of the Bruce Lee Family Archive

CHAPTER 10
Oakland

THE BOOK BRUCE was working on came out toward the end of the year, the first and only book finished by him.[78] In later years he supposedly asked the publisher to cease production because it gave the impression that he was advocating traditional *gung fu*, but at the time he was immensely proud of being a published author.[79]

Not long after Christmas, Bruce and Linda drove to Oakland to pick up James Lee, then drove on down to Pasadena to visit Ed Parker. Linda told her parents she was going down to see the Huskies in the Rose Bowl on New Year's Day with friends, but she never made it to the game. According to Linda, Bruce "couldn't care less" about football.

On the trip, Bruce picked up a batch of the newly-minted books.[80] I have no recollection of his touting the upcoming book in class, but I returned to school at the end of Christmas break. Undoubtedly he showed the book to the class after he got back.

The year had been an eventful one for Bruce, but the coming year, 1964, the second Year of the Dragon since Bruce was born, was to be momentous. His plan was to drop out of the University of Washington and move down to Oakland to start a new school with James. As the new year progressed, he talked to James Lee often over the phone and groomed Taky to take over the Seattle school. At the same time, he and Linda's relationship became more serious.

Meanwhile, my sophomore year at Yale seemed as bleak as the first. I had considered dropping out after freshman year, but inertia had borne me back. I was taking a second year of Chinese as well as first-year Japanese (both intensive), plus Chinese history and a math class (n-dimensional projective geometry). Fortunately, the Japanese class had an unintended marvelous consequence.

One day our Japanese instructor came into class carrying a letter. Shaking his head, he set it on the table and indicated we should read it. One by one we read the letter and passed it on. There were only five of us in the class. I was the last.

The letter was ostensibly written by a Japanese student at Vassar, then an all-girls school. According to the letter, she had heard Yale had a good Japanese language department and wanted to invite someone up to Vassar for the Junior Prom to spend a Japanese-speaking weekend. The other four guys in the class were graduate students who were already married or in a serious relationship. I was the only young unattached guy with raging hormones. I slipped the letter in my pocket and said I'd take care of it. I answered the letter, hitched a ride to Vassar for the prom and met my future wife, Noriko Goto.

As it turned out, the letter had been written as a prank by friends of Noriko. When she received my reply, accepting the offer, she already had a date for the prom. But she cancelled that date, and when I arrived played the gracious hostess for the weekend.

That summer I went home to Seattle to earn some money for college (and pay my father back for my Hong Kong trip the summer before). Noriko got a job at the New York World's Fair. Shortly after I arrived in Seattle, Bruce was on his way to Oakland.

———

BRUCE MOVED TO Oakland in July, in time for Wally Jay's summer luau. The semi-annual affair complete with roasting pigs drew over a thousand people, including many from the martial arts community, and helped fund trips his judo students took to matches and tournaments in other cities. With James Lee's prompting, Bruce had been invited to give a demonstration. Knowing what to expect, James sat back and watched with amusement.

Bruce's performance was by all accounts electrifying but at the same time polarizing. His one-inch punch and speed at closing the gap awed many in the crowd. But his explicit and detailed criticism of traditional *gung fu* styles apparently turned off many others.[81]

Bruce began teaching in James's garage, and soon thereafter they opened a Jun Fan Gung Fu Institute in new space. Bruce was still thinking of opening up a chain of schools, *a la* Ed Parker. Taky had been left running the original school, in Seattle. This was the second. Then came the month of August.

Early in the month, Ed Parker held his first Long Beach International Karate Championships, which he had been planning for nearly two years. The official program lists a number of "world renown experts [sic]" who would be giving demonstrations, including Bruce (billed as a "master of Gung Fu from Hong Kong, China"), Jhoon Rhee (a "gifted aerial kicker") and Ed Parker himself ("one of the pioneers of Karate in the United States").

Bruce was shepherded around by Dan Inosanto, one of Ed Parker's students who was competing in the tournament. In addition to karate, Dan was an expert in *escrima*, the Filipino martial arts which uses sticks and other weapons, as well as *nunchaku*. Impressed by the demo, Dan spent time with Bruce after the event and was "flabbergasted" by the way Bruce could control him.[82]

Bruce's performance was similar to the one he gave at Wally Jay's luau, but in front of a much larger crowd packed with luminaries not only from the martial arts community but also Hollywood. Unbeknownst to him at the time, his performance started a chain of events which led to his moving yet further south, to Los Angeles.

At the same time, although he was physically in the Bay Area, he was spending a lot of time on the telephone with Linda. She was pregnant, and they decided to get married. Since they knew her parents would not approve, the original plan was to elope, and he flew up to Seattle. But the news slipped out, so they agreed to attend an urgent family conference that had been called. Bruce hoped to obtain her parents' blessing. He didn't get it.

Her parents had not known that Linda was seeing Bruce, and their stance against interracial liaisons hadn't changed. The fact that she was pregnant did not sway them. Only when Linda refused to back down did the family reluctantly acquiesce. They were married August 17, 1964 in a hastily-arranged service in Seattle's Congregational Church. Taky was best man, the only non-family member in attendance.

———

AROUND THE SAME time, Noriko was in a serious car accident in New York and spent a while in the hospital. Since she wasn't able to return to work, my family invited her out to spend the rest of the summer with us. At some point I introduced her to Bruce when he was in Seattle.

Bruce was in full Bruce mode. Noriko was not a martial artist, and not particularly interested in the subject. In addition to expositions on *gung fu*, he explained his method for "training" women to her.[83] She was not impressed. She thought he was arrogant, self-centered and chauvinistic. How did I put up with him?

That was a question I sometimes asked myself. He liked the limelight and had a tendency to suck all the oxygen out of the room. He grew bored easily if the conversation was not focused on one of the few subjects he was interested in.[84] For me, though, he possessed knowledge I desperately wanted to learn. Letting him be the center of attention was the price of admission; and to me, it was a small price to pay. Every time I saw him on a break from college he had something radically new to show, grafted onto his existing skills as an organic extension, and the new revelations kept me in thrall.

One time it was his broken-rhythm technique. To demonstrate, he asked me to block a punch. At full speed there was no way I could block his punch, but this one he executed at half speed. It seemed to float out and I moved my hand for an easy block. But then the motion of his fist shimmered, as if an old-time movie film had snagged briefly before the reel resumed its revolution on the projector; the fist passed my hand right after the block and stopped an inch from my nose. Even after several tries I couldn't block the half-speed punch.

His evolving knowledge alone may or may not have been sufficient, but there were also two other factors. One, he was four years older than I was. As the oldest of four boys, I had no older brother, and perhaps subconsciously yearned for one. Bruce filled that role. Two, since I was away at college I was only sporadically in Seattle, and with Bruce spending more and more time in Oakland, there were fewer opportunities to get together.

As the years passed, Noriko's attitude changed. When we last saw Bruce, in Hong Kong less than a year before he died, she thought he had significantly matured.

SEVERAL DAYS AFTER they were married, Bruce and Linda flew to Oakland to move in with James Lee. Tragically, James's wife Katherine had been diagnosed with cancer and died a few weeks later. Linda helped take care of her and console James.

At the end of August, Bruce was slated to give a martial arts demonstration at Sun Sing Theater in San Francisco's Chinatown, the same theater where his father had performed two decades before around the time Bruce was born. Many in the Chinatown martial arts community showed up to see if the arrogant upstart would repeat the criticism of traditional *gung fu* which he had reportedly given at Wally Jay's luau and the Long Beach karate championships. He did not disappoint. His appearance supposedly led directly to the most well-known and controversial of Bruce's challenge matches, the one with Wong Jack Man.

The *gung fu* demonstration was an accompaniment to a cha-cha exhibition he gave with Diana Chang, a Hong Kong movie starlet, which was the main reason for his appearance. During his trip back to Hong Kong the previous summer, he had re-established some contacts in the Hong Kong movie industry, which eventually resulted in an engagement to accompany Diana on a promotional tour in California for her latest movie. Bruce accepted the job, but apparently only on the condition that he could also give *gung fu* demonstrations at the same time. He took Dan Inosanto along as his demo partner.[85]

One of the key things Bruce liked to focus on during his demos was closing the gap—the ability to close quickly from a distance beyond the opponent's range, before the opponent could react. He often asked for a volunteer from the audience for the demonstration. Apparently at Sun Sing the volunteer was able to block his strike, at least the first time. Accounts differ as to whether Bruce's strikes were repeatedly blocked by the volunteer, or whether it was only once, with Bruce overcompensating the second time and making actual contact. Personally, I find it unlikely that the volunteer was able to repeatedly block Bruce's strike. Those that could block even once were few and far between. And if someone could, why wouldn't he have used his broken-rhythm technique?

Accounts also differ as to his parting remarks at the end of the demonstration, and whether they were a direct challenge to San Francisco practitioners. One version of his remarks was that any time his "Chinese brothers" wanted to "research" his Wing Chun, they were welcome to find him at his school in Oakland. Others recall a more direct challenge. Bruce was trying to recruit students then for his new school, but he was also a master at artful phrasing that could be interpreted in wildly different ways. It is plausible to me that he phrased his remarks as an invitation to prospective students to observe his school, but in a way that a potential challenger could take as a thrown gauntlet.[86]

IT IS NOT disputed that in the aftermath of Bruce's demonstration at the Sun Sing Theater, a challenge from Wong Jack Man was delivered to Bruce in Oakland, that Bruce accepted, and that after lengthy negotiations as to time and place, Wong and five cohorts arrived at Bruce's Oakland school for the match in early November, 1964. But the reason for the challenge and the details of the fight itself—from the opening move, to how the fight ensued and its conclusion—remain a matter of controversy. With various versions of the encounter, some recounted by people who were not there,[87] it retains a *Rashomon*-like aura. I was not there either, but I have heard first-hand accounts from two people who were—Bruce and his wife Linda—and I have my own thoughts on what might have transpired.

The two competing reasons given for the challenge are because Bruce was teaching *gung fu* to non-Chinese, and the San Francisco martial arts establishment wanted him to stop; and that Bruce's comments at the Sun Sing Theater had insulted enough of the San Francisco martial arts community that some felt the insult needed to be avenged. The two versions are not necessarily mutually exclusive.

I don't recall ever hearing Bruce give the reason for the challenge. Linda believes that it was made to force Bruce to close his school. She was told that by Bruce. Matthew Polly surmises that Bruce may have told her that because it sounded better than the actual reason; he points out that by 1964 some *gung fu* schools in San Francisco taught non-Chinese, and no one tried to shut them down.[88] And Bruce's commentary at the Sun Sing Theater, featuring his cutting criticisms of classical *gung fu*, no doubt ticked off a lot of people. But Bruce's teaching of non-Chinese may well have exacerbated the ill will. Teaching a few non-Chinese as part of a mainly Chinese class is one thing; teaching openly to a class of mostly non-Chinese was something else. I can attest to the strong feelings that Bruce's teaching non-Chinese could stir up. The fact that he gave his demo at Sun Sing with Dan Inosanto, highlighting the fact that he was teaching non-Chinese, may have rubbed it in. It is hard for me to believe that Bruce's teaching of non-Chinese was not a contributing factor to the challenge.

When Wong Jack Man and his cohorts showed up on the appointed day, they were met by Bruce, Linda and James Lee. One account claims that James locked the front door after Wong's group entered, then retired to the rear of the studio where he kept a concealed handgun "in case the situation spun out of hand."[89] I doubt that. But according to Jesse, the thought passed through Bruce's mind as to whether he and James could win if Wong's cohorts joined the fight.[90]

Wong's group sought to establish some ground rules for the match, such as no groin kicks or hits to the head, but Bruce insisted on an all-out match. From this point forward, the versions of the fight itself differ in major respects.

The first blow was apparently thrown by Bruce, but there's disagreement about whether it was a punch or an eye-jab. Polly asserts it was a "four-finger spear" straight at Wong's eyes.[91] But the only person who claimed it was an eye-jab was apparently Wong himself. In his notes Polly acknowledges that one of Wong's contingent, David Chin, remembered it as a punch, but concludes that Wong's version is correct because finger jabs were "one of Bruce's favorite techniques" that he "practiced. . . relentlessly," and that they were an excellent attack against a taller opponent such as Wong.[92]

Linda, as well as David Chin, remembers Bruce's first blow as a punch. Bruce's own account to me was the same. As for Polly's surmise, it is true that Bruce considered eye jabs to be an important part of his all-around arsenal, and that he practiced them a lot. But he practiced two-finger jabs, not "four-finger spears." More importantly, the fact that he practiced them doesn't mean he used them in actual fights, even those proclaimed to be without rules. I have never heard of him using an eye-jab in a fight, in Hong Kong when he fought all the time or in later encounters in the States, including his fight with the karate challenger in Seattle. I have no doubt he would have used an eye-jab if he thought he was fighting for his life, but he had no reason then to think that he was. He had faced many more fearsome opponents before. I believe that Bruce closed the gap and opened with a series of straight punches.[93]

After Bruce's opening flurry of punches, all but Wong (including one of his cohorts) agree that he back-pedaled and then turned and ran, with Bruce chasing him from one room to the next and back again through connecting doors.[94] Bruce humorously recounted the fight to me years later, with Wong running and Bruce chasing behind, trying to punch the back of his retreating head. He told the same story to Jesse Glover.[95]

One claim of Wong's is that he had Bruce in a headlock at one point and refrained from delivering a killing blow. But no one else who was there, including his cohorts, supports that claim.[96]

More uncertain perhaps, but not in my mind, is whether Wong "yielded." All (except Wong) agree that he was on his back, with Bruce on top of him, asking him if he gave up. Bruce himself told me that when he finally caught up with Wong and took him to the ground, he was winded; he laughed as he reenacted how he held a fist over Wong's face, panting, and demanded that he yield. He said he was glad Wong did, since he didn't have much energy left to punch.

One version claims that Wong may have tripped as he was back-pedaling, and that although Bruce was on top of him demanding that he give up, he never actually did.[97] But it is hard for me to believe that Bruce would have let Wong up without punching him unconscious if he didn't yield, even if only by nodding his head. Linda is adamant that he yielded.

A recent detail that I never heard before is that Wong wore leather bracelets with wrist spikes to the match, concealed by his long sleeves. In this version, while he was running from Bruce he suddenly stopped and windmilled a karate chop to Bruce's neck, drawing blood.[98] Linda has no recollection of any wrist spikes, let alone of them drawing any blood. Since this detail apparently comes from one of Wong's cohorts, it is surprising to hear it, especially since if true it would have been an egregious breach of the accepted rules of engagement and reflected very unfavorably on Wong. It is doubly surprising since, according to Wong's version of the match, their understanding, at least when they arrived, was that it was supposed to be a "friendly" one.

The entire fight lasted only three minutes, but Bruce was out of gas. He was frustrated that the fight had lasted so long, that he hadn't been able to dispatch his opponent more quickly and efficiently. He played the fight over and over in his mind. He had already been thinking about a new approach to the martial arts, but the Wong Jack Man fight accelerated his thoughts. He determined to pay greater attention to stamina as an important factor in a fight and began running regularly.[99]

Sometime after the fight, Bruce and Linda were in San Francisco Chinatown on other business. The restaurant where Wong Jack man worked as a waiter was nearby. On a whim, Bruce suggested they swing by and pay a visit. They stood on the sidewalk and peered through the window. In Linda's words, Wong was in the process of pouring tea for a customer when he spotted Bruce. The tea he was pouring overflowed the cup and spilled all over the table. Bruce and Linda continued on their way.[100]

ENDNOTES

78 He wrote extensive notes, some of which were published after his death as *Bruce Lee: The Tao of Gung Fu*, edited by John Little, and *The Tao of Jeet Kune Do*, but never completed another book.

79 Polly, *A Life*, p. 134. When I spoke to her Linda did not recall him ever asking the publisher to cease publishing, since the book was self-published.

80 Gong, *The Evolution of a Martial Artist*, p. 49; Russo, *Striking Distance*, p. 103.

81 Polly, *A Life*, pp. 135-136.

82 Russo, *Striking Distance*, p. 116.

83 He sometimes liked to expound on how he "trained" women with his incremental demands. First step, "Could you please get me a cup of tea?" The next time, "Tea, please." Then, "Tea!" After which, supposedly, the tea would be brought without his having to ask. Like many guys, I'm sure his big talk vastly exceeded the reality.

84 Jesse Glover has written that when he hung out with Bruce his conversation always dealt with one of three topics—*gung fu*, Hong Kong or the cha-cha. Glover, *Bruce Lee*, p. 18.

85 Russo, *Striking Distance*, pp. 126-129.

86 See Polly, *A Life*, pp. 148-151, and Russo, *Striking Distance*, pp. 126-134, for a thorough discussion of the Sun Sing demo.

87 See, e.g., Polly, *A Life*, pp. 155-157, and Russo, *Striking Distance*, pp. 137-141.

88 Polly, *A Life*, notes to p. 154, on pp. 533-534.

89 Ibid., p. 154, citing Russo, *Striking Distance*, p. 137. However, it is not clear what Russo's source was for that claim. Linda says it is total nonsense.

90 Glover, *Bruce Lee*, p. 73. Another thing Bruce told Jesse was that he was pissed that the fight was taking place in front of his wife. If that was the case, it casts doubt as to whether the details for the challenge had been completely agreed upon.

91 Polly, *A Life*, pp. 155 and 201.

92 Ibid., notes to p. 155 on p. 534.

93 Wong apparently also later claimed that he was reaching out to shake hands ("touch gloves") as a matter of sportsmanship when Bruce suddenly launched a finger jab at his eyes. Polly, *A Life*, p. 155. I find that hard to believe, too. For one thing, shaking hands was not common in *gung fu* matches of the sort they were about to have ("touching gloves" is a boxing term). Further, the atmosphere in the room was by all accounts too tense by then for such a formality. Linda remembers at most a nod or bow before Bruce leapt forward and loosed a series of punches.

94 Ibid., p. 156 and notes thereto on p. 534.

95 Bax, *Number One*, pp. 20-21 and 89-90; Glover, *Bruce Lee*, p. 73.

96 Polly, *A Life*, notes to p. 156 on p. 535, calling it the "phantom headlock."

97 E.g., Polly states that Wong's cohorts intervened while Bruce was raining punches down on him, and pulled Wong "dazed and confused from the ground," but that Wong never said he gave up, apparently relying on a 2014 interview with David Chin. Polly, *A Life*, p. 157. Russo, in *Striking Distance*, p. 141, however, citing an earlier (2011) interview with David Chin, states that Wong gave up.

98 Polly, *A Life*, p. 156, citing David Chin.

99 In a September 1964 letter to Taky, before the Wong Jack Man fight, Bruce wrote that he was devising a "structure of my own principle using Wing Chun as foundation and my boundary lines as the skeleton." Gong, *The Evolution of a Martial Artist*, p. 84. For Bruce's reaction to the fight, see Linda Lee, *The Bruce Lee Story*, pp. 53-54. Linda attests that he began running regularly thereafter, as do his daytimers.

100 Polly states that Bruce paid Wong a visit a week after the match to smooth things over, reciting a long soliloquy which Bruce allegedly delivered. Supposedly Wong, sporting a black eye, refused to respond and Bruce eventually walked away. Polly, *A Life*, pp. 157-158. The citation for this story is unclear. Linda says that no such encounter occurred. To me, Linda's account of their visit to Wong's restaurant sounds more like Bruce. Bruce also told a similar story to Jesse. See Glover, *Bruce Lee*, p. 73.

Bruce and Linda
Courtesy of the Bruce Lee Family Archive

CHAPTER 11
Hollywood Calls

F 1964 WAS a momentous year, 1965 was in limbo. The year started on two high points, then slid sideways. The first high point was a call out of the blue from Hollywood. The second was the birth of Bruce and Linda's son Brandon.

The call came to James Lee's house in Oakland in late January from William Dozier, a Hollywood TV producer. He was developing a series to be called *Charlie Chan's Number One Son*, chronicling the quest of the fictional detective's son to avenge his father's murder. Dozier wanted to cast an Asian actor for the role, a radical idea in Hollywood then.[101]

Dozier was having trouble casting the right person for the part. Then he heard about Bruce's demo at the Long Beach karate championships the previous August, from Jay Sebring, a Hollywood hair stylist who had seen the performance. Sebring, who was later one of the victims of the Sharon Tate murders by the Charles Manson gang, was a nexus for Hollywood gossip. Bruce hadn't been thinking of Hollywood at all at that point. But the opportunity was too great to pass up. He agreed to fly down for a screen test, with Linda on the verge of giving birth.[102]

Brandon was born on February 1. Three days later, Bruce flew down to Los Angeles for the screen test. He was nervous and stuttered, but still charismatic.[103]

Almost immediately after returning to Oakland, he received the news that his father had died. He sent Linda and Brandon to Seattle to stay with Linda's parents, then flew back to Hong Kong for the funeral. Her mother's attitude toward Linda's marriage hadn't changed much with the birth of her grandchild. Bruce stayed in Hong Kong for three weeks and fulfilled the customary duties of a grieving son, returning to Oakland in March.[104]

Back in Oakland, he got another call from Dozier. Dozier wanted him for the part in the series. When the shooting would start was up in the air; it was supposed to take a few months for plans to jell. He offered Bruce a retainer of $1,800 for a one-year option, to keep him on board. Bruce didn't hesitate. The Oakland school hadn't done as well as Bruce and James had hoped, mainly due to Bruce's desire to teach only "serious learners."[105] Meanwhile, he continued to work on his new martial arts system, describing it in a letter to Taky as having "Wing Chun [as] the starting point, chi sao [as] the nucleus, and supplemented by the FIVE WAYS."[106]

With the schedule for *Number One Son* still uncertain, Bruce decided to use the option money to take Linda and Brandon to Hong Kong and introduce them to his family. He planned to return as soon as the project was ready to start.[107] Conditions were cramped and it wasn't easy for Linda, who spoke no Cantonese, but they ended up staying there for four months until they received word that the project had been postponed.[108] While there, Bruce continued to brood over the Wong Jack Man fight and outline ideas for his new system, which by then he described as being based on Wing Chun, fencing and boxing.[109] He also used the time to sound out movie contacts there, as a backup,[110] and to take over a hundred pictures of Yip Man doing Wing Chun forms.[111]

In September, Bruce and Linda headed to Seattle and moved in with Linda's family, initially expecting it to be brief, until the Hollywood opportunity solidified. But the months continued to drag on. The pressure on Bruce and Linda must have been tremendous. One can only imagine the comments from her parents as the weeks became months, Bruce with no job (and the option money from Dozier long spent), hanging around the house with nothing to do except read, take notes and practice *gung fu*. Sometime in late December or early January, they moved back down to Oakland, moving in with James Lee again, still hoping the TV series was about to become a reality.[112]

———————

AFTER GRADUATING FROM Vassar in June of 1965, Noriko started working at Canon Camera in New York City. I roofed for the summer in Peoria, Illinois, my brothers and I staying with an aunt and uncle while our parents took a trip to Europe. At the end of the summer I returned to New Haven for my senior year at Yale.

In December, over Christmas break, Noriko and I flew briefly to Seattle to get married. My parents weren't happy about it, arguing that I should finish school first. I acknowledged the reasonableness of their position, but the commute between New Haven and New York had become tiresome. Every weekend, either I took the train down to New York or Noriko took the train up to New Haven. By then she had an apartment of her own near the Hayden Planetarium, and we figured it would be a lot more economical if we got married and she moved up to New Haven.

We were married by a judge my father knew in the judge's chambers, with just the family present. We held a small reception for friends. Bruce and Linda may have still been in Seattle then, before moving down to Oakland, but I don't think I knew they were there.

IN EARLY 1966, when my brother Mike was a sophomore at Stanford and starting to box seriously, he visited Bruce in Oakland. They spent time watching boxing films, which Bruce played with running commentary. Sometimes he would back up the film and play it in slow motion, saying, "Watch this again, Mike." Mike recalls watching films of Joe Louis, Max Baer and Jack Dempsey. Dempsey was one of Bruce's favorites; they watched him knocking Jess Willard down in the first round with a left hook.

Stanford was then a member of the California Collegiate Boxing Conference, which included the University of Nevada and sometimes a Navy boxing team. Mike boxed for Stanford in his junior year, winning four out of six fights (two by KO) and losing two by decision. He trained and was in a lot better shape than I was, but still had a hard time in the third round.

In early March, the TV network rejected *Number One Son*, the first of a series of disappointments Bruce encountered in Hollywood due to its timidity in casting an Asian actor in a lead role. Instead, Dozier pitched Bruce on the role of Kato in *The Green Hornet*, another project Dozier had been working on.[113] Shortly thereafter, Bruce and Linda moved out of James Lee's house and down to a small apartment in Los Angeles, the first home they occupied on their own.[114]

Bruce promptly enrolled in acting lessons three times a week, paid for by 20th Century Fox. In a letter to Fred Sato, a Seattle judo man from whom Bruce learned some judo, he described the lessons in terms similar to those he used to describe his approach to the martial arts: "The lessons. . . [are] doing me a lot of good and [are making me] more fluid with not-acting acting—a most difficult way to achieve unnatural naturalness."[115]

———

THE FILMING OF *The Green Hornet* started in June of 1966, just after I graduated from college. I worked in New Haven that summer, hauling scrap metal in a scrap metal factory, while Noriko worked at the Yale Library. In the fall, I started at Harvard Law School, just as *The Green Hornet* began to air. We drove up from New Haven in the first car I ever owned, which barely made it for the short trip to Boston.

The Green Hornet ran for 26 episodes through March of 1967, with an additional two-part show teamed up with Batman and Robin. It did not garner any Emmys. But Bruce, despite his initial misgivings about playing a subservient role to Van Williams's Green Hornet, created some buzz.[116] Lanston Chinn, who had some *gung fu* under his belt from his time with Bruce, was then working as a social worker in Harlem. He stood out as a Chinese guy in a predominantly black neighborhood, but managed to project a Bruce Lee swagger that served him well. In just a short time, Bruce had started to change the perception of the Asian male in the American mind.

After *The Green Hornet* series ended, pickings were slim. Not only were his earnings from the series drastically reduced, his invitations to give paid appearances as Kato dried up too.[117] The few bit parts Bruce was able to land, and other work thrown his way as a favor, were not enough to pay the bills. By February of 1967 he had opened his third *gung fu* school, in Los Angeles Chinatown, but like his first two it had no signage and did not advertise.

To make ends meet he began giving private lessons to movie and TV stars he was introduced to. Many of the leading Hollywood actors prided themselves on being alpha males, and Asian martial arts were becoming very macho. Upon meeting Bruce, they realized he was the real deal. In August of 1967 he began giving private lessons to Steve McQueen.[118] In addition, he began giving private lessons to Mike Stone and Chuck Norris, two of the top U.S. karate men.[119]

In order to maintain his reputation in martial arts circles, he also made appearances at various tournaments. At Ed Parker's 1967 Long Beach karate championships in July, his appearance helped draw record crowds. But he was only willing to go so far to earn money off of his martial arts. He rejected a proposal from a businessman to underwrite a franchise of Kato self-defense schools.[120]

As 1968 started off, private lessons for Steve McQueen, Mike Stone and Chuck Norris continued, and lessons with karate man Joe Lewis began. Aside from giving private lessons to a few students, his daytimers for the first five months of the year leave the impression that he was mostly working out by himself, doing punches, stomach exercises, isometrics and various stretches.[121] He also ran and cycled for endurance. James Coburn and Roman Polanski were added as students later in the year. Director Blake Edwards (*Breakfast at Tiffany's, Pink Panther*) also at some point became a student, as did TV producer Sy Weintraub and casino magnate Beldon Katleman.[122]

One of Bruce's students was Stirling Silliphant, the well-known screenwriter/producer (he received an Oscar for *In the Heat of the Night*), who wangled an introduction to Bruce in March of 1968. Bruce initially hesitated to take Silliphant on as a student, telling him he was "too old" (he was then 50), but eventually relented. Silliphant became a Bruce devotee, and wrote Bruce into a bit part in *Marlowe*, a movie starring James Garner. Filming began in August, Bruce's first appearance in a full-length Hollywood film.[123]

IN OCTOBER OF 1968, my brother Mike was invited over for dinner by Bruce and Linda when Mike passed through Los Angeles. He had graduated from Stanford a few months before and was on his way to take a job with Vista on the Mescalaro Apache Reservation in New Mexico.

One of the things that Bruce was working on then was the force of his kicks. Jesse Glover has stated that Bruce's kicks "weren't much" when they first worked out together, and it was only later that his kicks became more powerful. At the time, it had never occurred to me that Bruce's kicks were less than devastating, but up until then Bruce had used them mainly to attack the shin, knee or groin, or as a distraction to close with an opponent. His attitude had begun to change early on in Seattle after he saw a karate demonstration in Tacoma by Hidetaka Nishiyama.[124] Jhoon Rhee has taken credit for giving Bruce pointers that helped increase his kicking power even more, while acknowledging that with only a little practice Bruce was able to generate a stronger kick than Jhoon Rhee himself.[125]

Bruce wanted to show Mike his "new kick." He had Mike hold a blocking dummy, which he kicked at full force. In Mike's words, "One step, a hop, and then 'Boom!'" with a sidekick. Mike was impressed with the power of the kicks, which lifted him onto his toes and sent him back-pedaling into the wall.

As Mike was getting ready to leave, the doorbell rang, and Bruce asked Mike to get it. A towering black man about Mike's age stood in the doorway.

"Hi, I'm Lew Alcindor."

Lew Alcindor (he did not change his name to Kareem Abdul-Jabbar until 1971) was then starting his senior year at UCLA, where he had already led the UCLA team to two NCAA basketball championships and had been named as the Most Outstanding Player in both tournaments (1967 and 1968). He had recently started learning *aikido*, but had been introduced to Bruce and drawn to his approach. He and Bruce spoke for a short while. When they were finished, Bruce asked him to drive Mike back to where he was staying, at a friend's house.

Bruce had started giving Kareem lessons earlier that year, at the end of April.[126] Bruce had worked out with plenty of larger opponents before, from Jesse Glover to Al Novak and many others. Bruce went out of his way to train with larger opponents. But Kareem was in a class by himself. It is hard to envision the size difference between Kareem and Bruce just from the numbers—Kareem's 7'-2" versus Bruce's 5'-8". You have to see a photo to appreciate the discrepancy. The fight scenes in the movie Bruce had only filmed part of when he died, *The Game of Death*, are amazing—like David against Goliath.

It was trying to do *chi sau* with Kareem that moved Bruce to deemphasize *chi sau* even more. When he stuck with Kareem, Kareem's arms were so long Bruce couldn't reach him. As Bruce put it in a remark to Taky, it was hard "doing it with a guy 7'-2" looking at his bellybutton."[127]

WITH ROLES SUITABLE for Bruce few and far between, he decided to make his own opportunity. The idea he came up with was a philosophical movie about a martial artist's quest for self-understanding, called *The Silent Flute*. He invested a lot of time and energy on the project over a couple of years, but ultimately it proved to be another major disappointment.

He realized that in order to get the movie made he would have to play a supporting role. In early 1969, together with Stirling Silliphant, he approached Steve McQueen to play the lead. But

McQueen declined, on the grounds that the movie was designed just to be a vehicle to make Bruce a star. He said he didn't want to "carry Bruce on his back," a remark which seriously aggravated Bruce. Bruce then approached James Coburn, who agreed.[128] A desire to surpass McQueen as a superstar became a motivating factor for Bruce from that point forward.

One of the gigs thrown Bruce's way to help him pay his bills was the coordination of a fight scene in *A Walk in the Spring Rain*, a movie starring Ingrid Bergman and Anthony Quinn. The movie had been written by Silliphant, who had written in the fight scene just so he could hire Bruce, and was being filmed in Tennessee. Two local stuntmen resented the little Chinese guy brought in from the outside, so Silliphant decided they needed an attitude adjustment. He arranged for Bruce to demonstrate his "new kick," with them holding a kicking shield. One after the other, he sent them flying into a swimming pool and turned them into true believers.[129]

While he was away, Bruce's daughter Shannon was born, on April 19, 1969. The birth was to be induced, the date having been set ahead of time, but Linda says they needed the money and Bruce went off to where the film was being shot in Tennessee. A student of Bruce's picked her and Shannon up at the hospital and took them home. A note in Bruce's daytimer for the day records the time of birth, weight and length and that he called Linda.

———

I GRADUATED FROM law school in June of 1969. After the birth of our son in Seattle in August, Noriko and I and our ten-day-old son flew to Tokyo where I had taken a job in an international law firm. We named our son Colin Musashi. His middle name was taken from Miyamoto Musashi, the 17th century Japanese master swordsman who wrote *The Book of Five Rings*, one of the martial arts books in

Bruce's extensive library. I knew Bruce was still making his way in Hollywood, as far as I knew doing very well.

———

BRUCE KEPT PLUGGING away on *The Silent Flute* project. After some hesitation and unsuccessful attempts by other screenwriters, Silliphant finally agreed to write the script. He and Bruce and James Coburn met regularly to finish the script over a period of three months, starting in February of 1970.[130] But Bruce did take two breaks from work on the script. The first was to fly to Switzerland to give Roman Polanski some private lessons. The second was to fly with his son back to Hong Kong for a few weeks, his first visit back since he had introduced Linda and Brandon to his family five years before.

The reception he received in Hong Kong was overwhelming. Unbeknownst to him, *The Green Hornet* had recently aired on Hong Kong TV, and become so popular that it was nicknamed *The Kato Show*. He was asked to appear on talk shows and give impromptu demonstrations.[131] During the visit he had a "movie dinner" with childhood friend Unicorn Chan, and may have asked him to approach Run Run Shaw of Shaw Brothers film studios with a proposal for a film.[132] The visit was brief, but it gave him a glimpse of the potential Hong Kong had to offer. It may also have given a glimpse of Bruce to Raymond Chow, then struggling with his newly-established Golden Harvest studio to survive in a war with Run Run Shaw's movie empire.[133]

Run Run Shaw was the 1,000-pound gorilla in the Hong Kong movie business. When Raymond Chow left Shaw Brothers to set up Golden Harvest, he conceived of it as working closely with Shaw, but a bitter feud soon developed over Golden Harvest's poaching of an actor still under contract with Shaw, Jimmy Wang Yu, the star of the *One-Armed Swordsman* movies. Since Yu couldn't make a movie in Hong Kong for Golden Harvest, Raymond Chow sent him up to Tokyo and co-produced a movie with a Japanese film company. The movie featured Yu and one of the leading actors in Japan, Shintaro Katsu, who starred in the hugely popular *Zatoichi* Blind Swordsman movies. The joint production was called *Zatoichi Meets the One-Armed Swordsman*.[134]

On August 13 Bruce suffered a potentially crippling back injury, when he started to lift weights in the morning without properly warming up. The doctors told him he would never kick high again. With money now even harder to come by, Bruce unable to work and two young mouths to feed, Linda found a job working for an answering service from late afternoon until nearly midnight. It was hard for Bruce to take, and he became depressed. It was one of the lowest points in his life.[135]

The first three months of his recovery period were supposed to be bed rest, but he got up and out when he had to. Silliphant had been hired by Tom Tannenbaum, the head of Paramount TV, to adapt some mystery novels about a blind detective for a pilot show that could be turned into a series, named *Longstreet*. Silliphant was still trying to help Bruce out, and realized the show could be a vehicle to accelerate Bruce's career. He set a meeting up at the end of September for Bruce to meet Tannenbaum to discuss the project, which apparently went well.[136]

To his doctor's surprise, Bruce was back on his feet in five months, and to all outward appearances back to normal, albeit with a lot of pain which he tried to hide. At some point, he began taking Darvon (a combination of aspirin and propoxyphene, a mild opioid) for the pain.

In the meantime, he had kept pushing for *The Silent Flute*, and Silliphant pitched the idea to Warner Bros. The studio agreed to do the film, but only if blocked funds in India were used for the production costs. The studio's condition meant that the movie would have to be shot in India. At the end of January 1971, Bruce and Coburn and Silliphant flew to Bombay to scout locations and assess local resources.[137]

On the flight, Coburn discovered that some of Bruce's habits can be annoying. Never Sits Still was constantly punching or doing something with his hands to develop his wrists or forearms.[138] Bruce once told me that when he went to the bathroom and washed his hands, he never used a paper towel to dry them off—he flapped his hands vigorously back and forth until they were dry, to exercise his wrists. I remember that every time I wash my hands where there are no towels. In Coburn's case, Bruce occupied himself on the flight from Bombay to New Delhi by pounding one fist and then the other on a writing pad, until Coburn couldn't stand it anymore and complained.[139]

Unfortunately, the conditions for film production they found in India were dismal. Bruce tried to convince Coburn it could work, to no avail. Tensions grew, especially between Bruce and Coburn, as they scoured the country for a couple of weeks. After they got back to Los Angeles in the middle of February, Coburn nixed India and the project was essentially dead.[140]

Shortly thereafter, another friend of Bruce's, Fred Weintraub, an executive at Warner Bros., tried to help him with another project. Weintraub had earlier sold Warner Bros. on a film to be called *Kung Fu*, featuring a Eurasian Shaolin warrior-monk played by Bruce, roaming the Wild West and using his fists to survive in a cowboy culture, but it had been cancelled after new senior executives came on the scene. His latest proposal was for *Kelsey*, a series set in the late 18th century about a trapper searching for a path through the lands of the Mandan people in the Dakota territories. He conceived of the show as including a part for Bruce, but the project didn't go anywhere and was rejected around the end of April.[141]

By the beginning of spring, *The Silent Flute* was on life support; nothing else was imminent, and Bruce still needed money.[142] Maybe it was time to jiggle the fishing lines he had out in Hong Kong. His daytimers indicate a call he made to Hong Kong in mid–March, and that he wrote a letter to Unicorn Chan a few days later. More calls and letters to Hong Kong followed in April, May and June.

ENDNOTES

101 Polly, *A Life*, pp. 163-164.

102 Ibid., pp. 164-165.

103 Ibid., pp. 165-169.

104 Thomas, *Fighting Spirit*, p. 71; Polly, *A Life*, p. 170. Linda reports that when she arrived in Seattle with baby Brandon, her mother's first reaction was something like, "How could you bring a yellow baby home?" Her mother was a product of her time, but grew to love and appreciate Bruce and her grandchildren once she got to know them. Some of my relatives initially harbored similar attitudes. When I married Noriko, one of my uncles asked my father how he could let me marry a "flat-nosed Jap."

105 Linda Lee, *The Bruce Lee Story*, pp. 62, 71.

106 See February 1965 letter to Taky, Little, *Letters of the Dragon*, p. 44. The "five ways" were the five ways of attack. Gong, *The Evolution of a Martial Artist*, pp. 126-133.

107 In a May 28, 1965 letter to Taky, he wrote that he planned to stay in Hong Kong until 20th Century Fox notified him that actual shooting was to start, which he thought would be in another two months. Little, *Letters of the Dragon*, p. 55.

108 Linda Lee, *The Bruce Lee Story*, pp. 71-72.

109 Bruce's August 7, 1965 and July 31, 1965 letters to James Lee. Little, *Letters of the Dragon*, pp. 63 and 60.

110 Polly, *A Life*, p. 175.

111 Little, *Letters of the Dragon*, July 29, 1965 letter to James Lee, p. 58.

112 Linda Lee, *The Bruce Lee Story*, p. 72.

113 Polly, *A Life*, p. 181. It is not clear at what point Bruce became aware that *Number One Son* was dead and *Green Hornet* was a go. Linda recalls it as being around the time Bruce signed the option agreement. Linda, *The Bruce Lee Story*, p. 71.

114 Linda Lee, *The Bruce Lee Story*, p. 73.

115 Little, *Letters of the Dragon*, April 9, 1966 letter to Fred Sato, p. 69. The letter also names Steve McQueen, Paul Newman and Vic Damone as prospective students. Clearly Bruce was moving fast in Hollywood!

116 Except for Bruce's role, the series was critically panned. When the network decided to cancel the show, Dozier notified Bruce with a lame crack that epitomized the Hollywood stereotype of Asians at the time: "Confucius say, *Green Hornet* to buzz no more." Chunovic and the Bruce Lee Estate, *The Unseen Bruce Lee*, p. 37.

117 Polly, *A Life*, p. 217.

118 Bruce's daytimers note numerous lessons, training sessions and other get-togethers with McQueen, starting on August 19, 1967.

119 According to his daytimers, he began giving lessons to them toward the end of 1967. As top karate practitioners who were already winning tournaments, they liked to portray the sessions as mutual training workouts, but I don't think there is any doubt about who was training whom.

120 Gong, *The Evolution of a Martial Artist*, p. 106. Polly, in *A Life*, p. 217 and notes thereto on p. 552, documents that the proposed name of the chain may have been the "Kato Karate Schools," a name Bruce would certainly have rejected out of hand. According to Linda, Bruce didn't seriously consider the offer, even though it might have solved his money problems.

121 For example, a January 1968 daytimer entry records that he did 1,000 punches in the late morning, followed by exercises and stretches in the afternoon and evening. A letter to George Lee, a friend and student who constructed a lot of Bruce's special equipment, in January, noted that he was training an average of 2-1/2 hours per day. Little, *Letters of the Dragon*, p. 105.

122 Polly, *A Life*, p. 233.

123 Linda Lee, *The Bruce Lee Story*, p. 87; Polly, *A Life*, pp. 222-223, 249.

124 Glover, *Bruce Lee*, p. 58. Jesse recounts that after seeing Nishiyama's demo in 1960 or so, Bruce started training that same night to develop the kind of focus and control that he witnessed during the demo.

125 Rhee, *Bruce Lee and I*, pp. 124-125.

126 Bruce's daytimers record Kareem's first lesson as April 30, 1968.

127 Gong, *The Evolution of a Martial Artist*, p. 112.

128 Thomas, *Fighting Spirit*, pp. 108-109.

129 Linda Lee, *The Bruce Lee Story*, pp. 85-86; Polly, *A Life*, pp. 263-264.

130 Linda Lee, *The Bruce Lee Story*, p. 90; Polly, *A Life*, p. 268. Bruce's daytimer records mid-February as the first script meeting.

131 Linda Lee, *The Bruce Lee Story*, pp. 95-96.

132 Thomas, *Fighting Spirit*, p. 117. Bruce's daytimers show a "movie dinner" with "Unicorn," presumably Unicorn Chan, who worked for the Shaw Brothers, on March 31, and a lunch meeting with a "Mr. Shaw" on April 11.

133 See Polly, *A Life*, p. 294. If Bruce didn't come to Chow's attention during his short stay in Hong Kong, it was no doubt in the aftermath, when Hong Kong media would call Bruce in Los Angeles in the early morning and broadcast the conversation live. Thomas, *Fighting Spirit*, p. 123; Linda Lee, *The Bruce Lee Story*, p. 96.

134 Polly, *A Life*, p. 301.

135 Polly, *A Life*, p. 269-271; Linda Lee, *The Bruce Lee Story*, pp. 88-89, 94-95; Gong, *The Evolution of a Martial Artist*, p. 116; Thomas, *Fighting Spirit*, pp. 113-114. Apparently he had had some back problems before—his December 10, 1968 and May 31, 1970 daytimer entries indicate that he had hurt his back then, albeit presumably not as seriously.

136 Gong, *The Evolution of a Martial Artist*, p. 116; Polly, *A Life*, p. 282.

137 Linda Lee, *The Bruce Lee Story*, pp. 90-92; Thomas, *Fighting Spirit*, p. 111; Polly, *A Life*, p. 272.

138 Jhoon Rhee, *Bruce Lee and I*, p. 75. Linda confirms that Bruce was "always doing more than one thing at a time." Even while reading, he would do stretches or punch a bag.

139 Linda Lee, *The Man Only I Knew*, p. 24.

140 Thomas, *Fighting Spirit*, pp. 111-113; Polly, *A Life*, pp. 272-275.

141 Polly, *A Life*, pp. 279-281.

142 The *Longstreet* pilot had aired, on February 23, 1971, but the project hadn't heated up yet. Polly, *A Life*, p. 282.

CHAPTER 12

Hedging Bets

THE FIRST FIRM offer Bruce received from Hong Kong was from Run Run Shaw. It was standard Shaw, a counter to an earlier proposal Bruce had made, a long-term contract at $2,000 per picture.[143] Although Hollywood thought Bruce was "too different" from its Asian stereotypes, Shaw viewed him the same as all the other Mandarin martial arts actors in his stable.

But Bruce's proposal had contained other stipulations that were important to him—the right to make script changes and total control over fight choreography—which Shaw had ignored.[144] Shaw's paternalistic response to Bruce's query about his other stipulations pissed him off.[145]

Raymond Chow of Golden Harvest, on the other hand, was patient and persistent. He and Bruce had talked, but up to then Bruce was still focused on Hollywood. This time Chow sent an emissary, the wife of Lo Wei, one of his top directors, to approach Bruce in Los Angeles. The offer wasn't great, $7,500 per picture, but it was better than Shaw's offer, and was only for two pictures versus the long-term contract Shaw wanted.

Golden Harvest's movies, as well as Shaw's, were all in Mandarin. Bruce's Mandarin was marginal, but the movies would be dubbed anyway. Before signing the contract with Golden Harvest, Bruce watched a number of Mandarin martial arts movies, which he thought were awful.[146] He signed the contract on June 28, 1971, perhaps against Coburn and Silliphant's advice.[147] But he needed the money more than ever. Their financial problems and the fact that Linda was still working, which Bruce didn't like, were the motivating factors.[148]

Filming for the one *Longstreet* episode in which Bruce was to appear took place in late June and early July. The film turned out to be Bruce's best work to date, and showcased his philosophical as well as practical approach to the martial arts. A few days after the filming was finished, he hopped a plane for Hong Kong, en route to shoot his first movie for Raymond Chow. Chow had wanted him to fly directly to Thailand, lest Run Run Shaw try to entice him away from Golden Harvest, but Bruce refused.[149] When he took off, he apparently still held out hope that *The Silent Flute* would come through.[150]

The first movie was *The Big Boss*. Preproduction had already started, with James Tien cast as the lead. Bruce was a late-hour addition. The plot revolved around Chinese workers in an ice factory used to front a drug-smuggling operation run by Thai gangsters. Bruce's role as a newly-arrived country bumpkin, trying to make a new life in Thailand, was inserted into the plot line.[151] Before Bruce left for Thailand, Linda quit her job.[152]

SHOOTING CONDITIONS IN Thailand were primitive. The film location was in a small village north of Bangkok, at the height of a hot, humid summer. In his first letter home to Linda he complained of the mosquitoes and cockroaches.

The cockroaches may have been more than just an annoyance to Bruce. The one phobia I ever saw him manifest was over cockroaches. Whenever one made an appearance the summer I was staying with his family, he would go wild, smashing it in almost a frenzy with a rolled-up newspaper. It seemed his aversion hadn't diminished much over the years.[153]

He also suffered other minor mishaps. As a result of the lousy food and unclean water, his weight dropped to 128 pounds; he cut his hand while washing a thin glass and required ten stitches. Later, he sprained an ankle and caught the flu. His back injury was also still giving him trouble.[154]

To top it off, relations with the lead actor, his friends among the crew and the film's directors were contentious from the start. James Tien was being paid a fraction of what this interloper was being paid. Bruce clashed with the first director over the fight scenes, which in traditional Mandarin martial arts movies were somewhat baroque. Bruce insisted they be more realistic. The first director, also on bad terms with many others on the set, was removed. Lo Wei was parachuted in to replace him. But Bruce's relationship with Lo Wei turned out to be no better, with numerous disputes.[155]

While *The Big Boss* was being shot, *Longstreet* was about to air in the States. Bruce had only been in one of the four episodes which had been filmed. Tom Tannenbaum, the head of Paramount TV, liked it so much that he wanted it to air first. The audience would naturally expect Bruce to be in more episodes, but he was not under contract.[156]

Tannenbaum tracked Bruce down in Thailand and a long-distance negotiation ensued via telegram, Bruce leveraging his Golden Harvest movies to demand higher compensation.[157] He agreed to take some time off after *The Big Boss* was wrapped up, fly to Los Angeles to shoot some more *Longstreet* episodes, then fly back to Hong Kong to film his second movie for Golden Harvest.[158]

———————

WHEN BRUCE GOT back to Los Angeles after filming *The Big Boss*, in early September, he heard that Weintraub had found a way to revive the *Kung Fu* project by converting it from a feature film into a TV series. Bruce desperately wanted the part, lobbying for it and pulling all the strings he had. But Hollywood was still too timorous. Its perception of what the American public would accept turned out to be an insurmountable barrier. The role was virtually designed for Bruce, but as Tom Kuhn, head of the Warner Bros. TV Division, put it, Bruce was "too authentic." He didn't seriously consider Bruce for the role, but Bruce wasn't told that right away.[159]

Ted Ashley, the chairman of Warner Bros. and also a student of Bruce's, agreed with Kuhn, but didn't want to lose Bruce. In October, Ashley offered him an enticing contract to develop his own show. Bruce proposed one he called *The Warrior*, similar in some respects to *Kung Fu*. His general plan at that point was to finish his two movies for Golden Harvest, then return to Los Angeles to pursue his TV opportunities there. Paramount TV also promised to develop a TV show for him.[160]

Meanwhile, Bruce filmed his bit parts in three more Longstreet episodes. Since the scripts had already been written, they had to be rewritten to shoehorn him in. He fought for more lines, but they were still few.[161] As the filming was taking place, the *Longstreet* premier aired and Bruce's part attracted rave reviews and a lot of fan mail.[162] Maybe if the timing had been different, he would have stayed in Hollywood. One can speculate whether that would have been better or worse for his career, though it is hard to imagine how his career path from that moment on could have been better.

As his scheduled return to Hong Kong grew closer, Bruce hadn't yet made up his mind about the offers from Warners and Paramount. James Coburn reiterated his consistent advice to Bruce to avoid TV series because they "chewed up geniuses," which may have been a factor.[163] And perhaps Bruce first wanted to see how *The Big Boss* did before signing any contract.

IN MID-OCTOBER, AFTER finishing the *Longstreet* episodes, Bruce and Linda and the kids flew to Hong Kong. Filming for *Fist of Fury*, the second of the two Golden Harvest movies Bruce had agreed to be in, was about to start, even before *The Big Boss* was released.[164]

Fist of Fury featured Bruce as the top student of a real-life Chinese martial artist who had captured his country's imagination early in the 1900s. The movie starts with Bruce's character arriving late for his master's funeral, the master having been poisoned by the head of a Japanese martial arts school. Japanese martial artists from the school show up at the burial with a mocking sign referring to China as the "Sick Man of Asia." Bruce returns the sign to the school, beats up everyone he finds there and rips up the sign, declaiming that "the Chinese are not the sick men of Asia!"[165]

The violence escalates as Bruce's character continues his search to uncover the identity of his master's murderer and avenge his death. Along the way, he demolishes the sign "No Dogs or Chinese Allowed" at a park entrance. After the climactic scene where he defeats the head of the Japanese school, he returns to find his friends at his own school slaughtered. He is surrounded by police and charges them with a flying kick, going out in a blaze of bullets, like Butch Cassidy and the Sundance Kid.[166]

The filming was to take place in Hong Kong, under better conditions than Thailand, but friction between Bruce and Lo Wei carried over. There was no script, only a rough outline. Shooting a film without a script was the norm for Lo Wei's movies, and had been the case for *The Big Boss*, but Bruce refused to start shooting without one.[167]

With the filming delayed, Bruce flew up to Tokyo to try to convince Shintaro Katsu, whose Blind Swordsman movies he had always enjoyed, to appear in the movie.[168] Although it may seem presumptuous to ask a leading Japanese actor to appear in a low-budget Hong Kong movie that featured the Japanese in a rather negative light, Bruce probably figured he had a chance because of Katsu's previous appearance in the co-production with Golden Harvest.

Bruce was not successful in obtaining Katsu for the film, but Katsu offered up two other Japanese actors who were agreeable. Upon arriving in Hong Kong, they were instructed to be as odious as they could be for the film. They knew the movie was anti-Japanese, but they weren't provided with a copy of the screenplay.[169]

I was working away in Tokyo while Bruce was meeting with Katsu, but our paths didn't cross. Less than half a year later, however, I would meet Katsu in a different deal involving Muhammad Ali.

———

BRUCE AND LINDA watched the midnight premier of *The Big Boss* on October 30, 1971, with great anticipation. Hong Kong moviegoers were notorious for being a tough audience, displaying displeasure with loud jeers and sometimes by carving up the theater seats with knives. But Bruce and Linda needn't have worried. When the movie ended, the crowd jumped to its feet with a rowdy standing ovation. Within three weeks, box office receipts smashed the previous record-holder, *The Sound of Music*. The low-budget, hastily-produced film was a runaway hit, not just in Hong but throughout the

Mandarin circuit in Southeast Asia and cities as far-flung as Rome, Beirut and Buenos Aires.[170]

In November of 1971, the role of the warrior-monk in *Kung Fu* was given to David Carradine, who was not only 100% Caucasian, but who at that time reportedly had a major drug problem and no background in Asian martial arts. On November 25, Bruce received an international phone call, informing him that he wouldn't be getting the *Kung Fu* role. At the same time, he was told that Warner Bros. wasn't going to do *The Warrior*.[171]

The disappointment was the straw that broke the camel's back. With *The Big Boss* doing well, Bruce decided to shift his eggs to the Hong Kong basket. He was doing better financially, but his house in Los Angeles was still a huge cash drain. By the first part of 1972, he had sold it.[172]

When shooting for *Fist of Fury* resumed, so did conflict with Lo Wei. Bruce won over the stuntmen, however, despite some initial resentment and rivalry, with a combination of prowess and generosity, sticking up for them and even paying their medical bills when the company didn't. He also brought over one of his Oakland students for the film, Bob Baker, to play the Russian villain (laying the groundwork for Caucasians to play the bad guys in future Hong Kong films), and highlighted the *nunchaku* for the first time in a full-length film. Shooting was completed in six weeks.[173]

One account of the making of *Fist of Fury* claims that Lo Wei had to pay "protection money" to local gangs for the use of their turf for some of the filming, and that Bruce had to be "restrained from attacking the hustlers."[174] This surprised me when I read it, especially recalling the way Bruce reacted to requests for "lucky money" in his earlier, more pugnacious days, when I stayed with him in Hong Kong. Linda says she hadn't heard that story, and that it "didn't ring true"—Bruce was not in "attack mode" then.

As shooting for *Fist of Fury* wrapped up, and months before its release, Bruce began thinking ahead to his next movie. He had completed his contract with Golden Harvest and was a "free man." He wanted control over the creative elements of the movie and formed a production company as a joint venture with Raymond Chow, Concord Productions Inc., profits to be split 50/50.[175]

The first movie Raymond Chow wanted to make under the new arrangement was one called *Yellow Faced Tiger*, to be directed by Lo Wei. Since the first two movies directed by Lo Wei and starring Bruce had been smash hits, why not a third? Shooting was scheduled to start in Japan in January of 1972. But drawn-out negotiations and bickering over the movie culminated in a final break with Lo Wei.[176]

ENDNOTES

143 Linda Lee, *The Man Only I Knew*, p. 134.

144 Thomas, *Fighting Spirit*, p. 119.

145 Linda Lee, *The Man Only I Knew*, p. 134.

146 Ibid., p. 135.

147 Bruce may have been advised to hold out for more money (Thomas, *Fighting Spirit*, p. 123), or because Golden Harvest was a risky start-up (Polly, *A Life*, p. 304).

148 Linda Lee, *The Bruce Lee Story*, p. 106. Linda doesn't know whether his buddies cautioned him against accepting Chow's offer, but confirms that they needed the money.

149 Thomas, *Fighting Spirit*, pp. 120-122, 124; Polly, *A Life*, p. 307.

150 In a July 1971 letter to a friend, he mentioned the "possible shooting" of *The Silent Flute* after his two pictures for Golden Harvest. Little, *Letters of the Dragon*, p. 147.

151 Thomas, *Fighting Spirit*, pp. 125-127; Polly, *A Life*, p. 307.

152 Linda Lee, *The Bruce Lee Story*, p. 106.

153 In his letter, he wrote that he could ignore the lizards, but referred to the cockroaches as a "constant threat." Little, *Letters of the Dragon*, p. 149. Others have written of an attack dog phobia Bruce supposedly had, as well as an aversion to swimming (Polly, *A Life*, p. 314; Thomas, *Fighting Spirit*, p. 125), but Linda says she has never heard of that.

154 Linda Lee, *The Bruce Lee Story*, pp. 102-103.

155 Thomas, *Fighting Spirit*, pp. 127-128; Polly, *A Life*, pp. 308-315.

156 Polly, *A Life*, p. 315.

157 In a letter to Linda describing the negotiation with Paramount, he wrote, "There comes a time when you have to advance or retreat—this time I can always retreat to my Hong Kong deal." Little, *Letters of the Dragon*, pp. 154-155.

158 Polly, *A Life*, p. 318; Linda Lee, *The Bruce Lee Story*, p. 106.

159 Polly, *A Life*, pp. 321-322, 324.

160 Ibid., pp. 326-327; Linda Lee, *The Bruce Lee Story*, p. 107.

161 Polly, *A Life*, pp. 318-319.

162 Thomas, *Fighting Spirit*, p. 128; Polly, *A Life*, pp. 320-321.

163 Linda Lee, *The Bruce Lee Story*, p. 107.

164 Thomas, *Fighting Spirit*, p. 133.

165 Polly, *A Life*, pp. 337-338.

166 Ibid., pp. 338-339; Thomas, *Fighting Spirit*, pp. 133-135, 138.

167 Polly, *A Life*, p. 337.

168 Ibid., p. 339. Linda recounts that Bruce took her to see Katsu's Blind Swordsman movies when they were dating.

169 Ibid., pp. 339-340.

170 Thomas, *Fighting Spirit*, pp. 129-131; Linda Lee, *The Bruce Lee Story*, pp. 107, 112.

171 Polly, *A Life*, pp. 325 and 334, citing Bruce's day-time planner. (The daytimer notes that Warner Bros. called, but does not describe the contents of the call. However, Polly's sequence of events seems likely.)

172 Linda Lee, *The Bruce Lee Story*, p. 106.

173 Polly, *A Life*, p. 346; Thomas, *Fighting Spirit*, pp. 135-136; Linda Lee, *The Bruce Lee Story*, p. 113. The *nunchaku* was used by Bruce briefly in the *Green Hornet*, but this movie marked its real introduction into film.

174 Thomas, *Fighting Spirit*, p. 136.

175 Ibid., p. 140; Polly, *A Life*, pp. 351-352.

176 Polly, *A Life*, pp. 358-361; Thomas, *Fighting Spirit*, p. 141.

Author and Bruce, Hong Kong, summer 1963

CHAPTER 13
A Meteoric Rise

B Y THE TIME Bruce broke with Lo Wei he had decided he wanted to direct his next film, ultimately named *Way of the Dragon*. But first he had to convince his partner Raymond Chow to let him direct the film, which would be his first directorial effort. He played Run Run Shaw off against Chow in order to get Chow's okay.[177]

In fact, Bruce intended not only to "write, produce, direct, and star in it," he intended to "scout the locations, cast it, choose the wardrobe, and choreograph the fight scenes." For good measure, he decided it would be the first Hong Kong-based picture to be shot in Europe, with its crowning fight scene to take place in "that ancient home of the gladiatorial arts, the Colosseum."[178] Needless to say, it was an ambitious undertaking.

Bruce already viewed his first two films as doing for him "what the spaghetti Westerns did for Clint Eastwood."[179] *Way of the Dragon* would be icing on the cake. He was still looking for a way back to Hollywood, but with the success of *The Big Boss* Hong Kong was looking more and more viable as a permanent base.

Author and Muhammad Ali, Tokyo, April 1972

Fist of Fury was released on March 22, 1972. Within four weeks, it had surpassed *The Big Boss* in receipts.[180] The following month, Stirling Silliphant happened to visit Hong Kong and Bruce made sure he saw the show in a theater with a Chinese audience. Silliphant, who still had hopes of making *The Silent Flute* a reality, was suitably impressed.[181]

———

I WAS STILL working in Tokyo when *Fist of Fury* was breaking records in Hong Kong. But I had no idea of that. Our second child, Kari Yukimi, was born on January 2, 1972, and between the office and my duties as a young father I was fully occupied. As far as I knew, Bruce was still in Los Angeles, trying to break into the movie business there.

In late March of 1972, Muhammad Ali came to Tokyo to fight Mac Foster. The firm I worked for, Adachi & Hayashida, represented a restauranteur/promoter named Rocky Aoki who was commissioned to drum up endorsements and other potential business deals for Ali in Japan. My boss, Jim Adachi, asked me to do the work.

Bruce never met Ali, but he studied Ali's fight films, even watching them in the mirror, so he could mimic Ali's movements with a right-hand lead.[182] And Ali later came to know of Bruce. They also had a lot of similarities: in addition to prodigious physical abilities, they both had a lively sense of humor and tremendous character. They chose their paths and kept to them, overcoming severe obstacles while sticking to their principles in order to do so. In Ali's case, his fight in Tokyo was during his comeback, after a three-and-a-half-year layoff imposed as a result of his refusal to be inducted into the army during the Vietnam War. A layoff at the height of his athletic prowess, which undoubtedly cost him millions of dollars in lost purses.

I was told that Ali was willing to promote almost any product except tobacco or alcohol. The only advertisement I recall him being in which showed in Japan was for Beaver Air Conditioning. But Shintaro Katsu, of the *Zatoichi* movies, whom Bruce had tried to obtain for his second film, was interested in doing a documentary of Ali. Rocky Aoki took me along for a dinner with Katsu and his wife, the actress Tamao Nakamura, and a deal was struck in concept, which involved a down payment of $50,000 to Ali for the right to use footage from some of his fights.

At that time in Japan it was necessary to obtain a government license in order to remit money overseas. Depending on the purpose of the remittance, the license was sometimes perfunctory but often involved lengthy negotiations with some bureaucrat in the Ministry of Finance. In the case of the down payment for the movie rights, there was apparently not enough time to obtain the necessary license and remit funds before the filming started, so arrangements were made to deliver cash in exchange for Ali's signature on an agreement.

A meeting was set up in one of the hotel rooms used by Ali and his entourage, who occupied most of one wing on one of the upper floors of the Hotel Okura, then the premier hotel in Tokyo. It was the evening before the fight. Bob Arum, who was acting as Ali's lawyer, was in the room, along with several tough-looking Black Muslims from Ali's entourage, wearing suits and sunglasses. Shintaro Katsu's lawyer, a Japanese lawyer from a different firm than mine, arrived shortly, along with several equally tough-looking Japanese who had the appearance of *yakuza* (Japanese gangsters). The Japanese were carrying a couple of small briefcases.

After the introductions, the *yakuza*-looking guys laid the briefcases on the bed, snapped them open and stepped back. The briefcases were filled with stacks of ten-thousand-yen bills (each bill then being worth approximately thirty dollars). Ali's guys dumped the money on the bed and started counting it. The Japanese stood back against the wall closest to the door and watched with crossed arms. It turned out that no one had prepared a contract, so Arum started to write one out long-hand on hotel stationery.

The contract wasn't overly elaborate, since it only took a few pages of writing. When he finished, Arum handed it to the Japanese lawyer to review. The Japanese lawyer stood there staring at the hand-written pages, a glazed expression on his face. My client's interest was just in receiving his commission, so I looked over the Japanese lawyer's shoulder to make sure that the commission was provided for.

The Japanese lawyer was still staring at the contract when Ali's guys finished counting the money, confirmed that it was the correct amount and stacked the bills back in the briefcases. They picked up the briefcases, whereupon the Japanese guys filed out of the room, followed by Ali's guys with the money. Arum announced that Ali wasn't back yet but would sign later once he returned. Then he left, too.

The Japanese lawyer and I waited for a while, but as time passed and no one seemed to know when Ali would return, we decided to leave. It was by then nearly midnight. Just as the Japanese lawyer and I began walking down the hall to the elevators, Ali emerged from an elevator and headed toward his suite at the end of the hall. "Howdy, Hoss," he said at me as he breezed by. As late as it was, with the fight the next day, no one suggested that we should try to get Ali's signature then.

As the elevator doors closed, a black guy with a friendly smile stepped in. He didn't seem to be a Black Muslim, so I assumed he was part of Ali's Louisville contingent. I nodded in the direction Ali had taken and asked if he trained this way for every fight. The guy chuckled and said, "He don't drink, and he don't smoke. But you put a piece a pussy in front of him, he take it."

Riding down in the elevator, the Japanese lawyer still held Arum's hand-written contract in one hand. He looked at me and asked in a tentative voice, "Do you think this is all right?" I assured him that Arum was a reputable lawyer and said I was confident it would work out. Myself, I was looking forward to the fight the following day, since I had been given a ringside ticket, and invited to the victory party afterwards (assuming Ali won, which was expected to be the case).

―――――

THE FIGHT THE next day, on April Fool's Day, wasn't one of Ali's best. It went the full distance, with Japanese fans yelling out in later rounds

"*Taose!* Knock him down!" But it was a unanimous decision, for Ali.

The victory party was held at Ali's hotel at the end of one of the corridors leading from the elevators, in a suite of rooms occupied by Ali's entourage. I called Noriko from the suite to invite her over. Although she professed to disdain boxing, she leapt at the chance.

Ali was still cleaning up after the fight as the guests who were waiting for him milled about. A couple of American hippie-types who were in Tokyo and had somehow learned of the party drifted down the corridor and approached the suite where everyone was gathered. A self-important member of Ali's entourage, a white guy from the East Coast whose function I don't recall, braced the two and curtly told them that it was a private party. The hippies drifted back towards the elevator bank and hung around in the vicinity.

At some point I exited the suite to walk to the elevators. Noriko and I lived a short cab ride away from the hotel, so I expected that she'd be arriving soon. As I reached the elevators, one of them stopped at the floor and the elevator door opened.

Ali jauntily strode out, sporting a few bumps and bruises on his face. He spotted the two hippies and immediately stopped to chat. After a brief exchange, he invited them to the party. Like Bruce, Ali went out of his way to befriend the little guy, rather than those in power.

For the rest of the evening, the hippies floated around the party as if on cloud nine. The guy who had initially banned them had a sour expression on his face. He reminded me of the L'il Abner character with a perpetual raincloud over his head, but since Ali himself had invited them in, he couldn't say a word.

When Noriko showed up and was introduced to Ali, she looked as awestruck as the hippies, remarking later that he was much bigger than she imagined. Years later I had a second occasion to interact with Ali, on a trip to Beijing.

BRUCE'S TEAM ARRIVED in Rome to film *Way of the Dragon* in early May of 1972. The shooting, including illegal filming in the Colosseum, was hectic, except for the fight scenes. Those, Bruce planned out meticulously and shot over and over until they were exactly what he wanted.[183]

Way of the Dragon was played as a comedy. As he had in *The Big Boss*, Bruce portrayed a country bumpkin who arrives in Rome to work, this time in a Chinese restaurant beset by an Italian mob which wanted the land. Once again, he highlighted the *nunchaku*, including a humorous scene where an Italian hood picks a set up and manages to knock himself out. Although like his first two films *Way of the Dragon* was originally intended to be for Chinese audiences in the Southeast Asian market, Bruce for the first time used Cantonese for the dialogue rather than Mandarin in the Hong Kong premier.[184]

He also for the first time imported real martial artists for the major fight scenes (a Korean *hapkido* expert and karate men Chuck Norris and Bob Wall), rather than use actors. In the final fight scene with Norris in the Colosseum, inspired by Ali's fight against Cleveland Williams, Norris gets the best of Bruce at first, but Bruce bounces back and begins dancing like Ali to gain the upper hand.[185]

Back in Hong Kong after shooting what they could in Rome, the press hounded Bruce to predict how *Way of the Dragon* would do at the box office. He didn't hesitate to respond, indicating that the movie would pull in five million dollars Hong Kong—topping both of his previous two movies, and over three times what *The Sound of Music* had grossed in Hong Kong.[186] Since the dialogue was in Cantonese, which he knew would go over especially well in Hong Kong, where the audiences had to read subtitles to the Mandarin films, no doubt he thought he had an edge.

<hr>

PRINCIPAL PHOTOGRAPHY FOR *Way of the Dragon* was finished at the end of July.[187] Almost immediately Bruce started working on *Game of Death*. He had no script, mainly just a vague idea for the film. The film would follow a group of five top martial artists who were hired to retrieve a stolen treasure from a five-story pagoda. Each level of the pagoda would be guarded by an expert martial artist embodying a different style, who had to be defeated in order to move up to the next level.[188]

Toward the end of August, Kareem Abdul-Jabbar happened to be in Hong Kong. Bruce conceived of Kareem as the guardian of the pagoda's top level, a master of "no style," and seized on the opportunity to film the scene with him first. Over the next month or so he also filmed scenes with Dan Inosanto, as an *escrima* master who guarded the third level, and Ji Han-Jae, a Korean *hapkido* expert who guarded the fourth level. He discussed bringing Taky Kimura over as the guardian of one of the levels, and considered his childhood Wing Chun teacher Wong Shun Leung as another, but the scenes of the top three levels were the only ones he was able to film before he got side-tracked with an offer from Hollywood—the one that truly made him an international phenomenon.[189]

<hr>

MY ORIGINAL COMMITMENT with the law firm in Tokyo was for three years, ending around the beginning of September, 1972. I enjoyed Japan, and as the third year drew to a close I extended for a fourth.

On October 19, 1972 I flew down from Tokyo to Hong Kong on business. Noriko had never been to Hong Kong before, so she accompanied me. As far as I knew, Bruce was still in Los Angeles, but I remembered his family with fondness and tried to look them up.

I visited the family apartment on Nathan Road where I had stayed nine years before, but it had been converted to a nursery school. No one knew where the Lee family had gone. I then looked up all the names of family and friends I could think of in the phone book, such as his brother Robert and Robert's cousin Tony Lai. No luck.

I had all but given up hope of making contact with Bruce's family, but the day before I was scheduled to fly back to Tokyo I happened to be meeting with a Chinese accountant in his office. After our business was over, I mentioned that I had been trying to find the family of an old friend of mine but hadn't been able to locate anyone.

He asked me the name of the friend. You wouldn't know the friend, I said. His name was Bruce Lee; he was living in Los Angeles. But the family was the family of a well-known Cantonese opera star, Lee Hoi Chuen.

The accountant looked at me skeptically. "You're an old friend, you say? Well, I don't think he's in Los Angeles."

As I stared at the accountant, he stood and picked up a newspaper from the coffee table I was sitting next to. He opened the paper to the movie section and folded it over to show me a full-page ad with a picture of Bruce delivering a flying kick. It was an ad for his second movie that had been released some months before, *Fist of Fury*. Lee Siu Lung, Lee Little Dragon, was the talk of the entire city. Apparently I was the only person in Hong Kong that thought he was still in Los Angeles.

I didn't expect that Bruce would be in the phone book, but I looked. There was actually one Bruce Lee listed, so I called the number. I was obviously not the first person who had called trying to reach the other Bruce Lee; he patiently explained that he was not the one I wanted.

I had a friend call a Chinese newspaper and ask the entertainment editor the name of the movie studio Bruce was associated with. Then we called the studio. They would not release his phone number, but if I left my name and number, they would pass it on. I gave the Chinese name Bruce had given me, *Baak Ma Dak*, White Horse Doug.

Five minutes later, the phone in our hotel room rang. "You son of a gun," Bruce yelled when I answered. "What are you doing in Hong Kong?"

He and Linda picked us up and took us back to the huge house he had recently bought in an exclusive part of town called Kowloon Tong, one of the few sections of Kowloon with single-family stand-alone houses. It wasn't the biggest house on the block, but it was impressive, surrounded by a high stone wall with broken glass or spikes on the top. In addition to the house, the wall enclosed a Japanese garden with a pond and arched bridge over it.

He had made it, but fame had its price. His children had to be escorted to and from school so they wouldn't be kidnapped. When Noriko had to use the toilet, Bruce produced a chain of keys to unlock the bathroom door. The house was then being renovated, and apparently he had to keep almost every room in the house locked to guard against theft by the workmen.

At one point as we sat in the living room Bruce looked through his mail. One of the letters was from James Lee in Oakland. I could see him frowning as he read the letter, then heard him whisper to Linda to send James $500. As I recall, Bruce told me later that James was dying of cancer.[190]

He also told me about an incident that had occurred a few months earlier on a benefit show for a charitable cause on TV.[191] He had been invited to appear on the show along with several other *gung fu* masters. One of the other masters was bragging about his "internal *qi*," his inner power, goading Bruce and challenging him to strike his stomach. The master stood in a ready stance, one arm at his side, the other pointing at his stomach, insisting that Bruce hit him there. Because of his internal *qi*, he said, it was impossible to hurt him. Bruce approached and the master insisted again. Bruce tapped him on the nose, not that hard but hard enough to smart. The master jumped back, startled and incensed, demanding to know what Bruce was doing. "Anyone can learn to resist a blow he is prepared for," Bruce recounted. "A *gung fu* man must be prepared for the unexpected."

Bruce and Linda invited us to stay with them, so we made arrangements to extend our stay and checked out of the hotel. That evening we went out to dinner. One thing that struck me was the casual clothes Bruce wore when we went out, including a sweatshirt. It was a contrast to the flashy clothes he had always favored. If it was an attempt to slip under the radar and avoid attention when he went out in public, it failed.

When we stopped for a light, people on the street or in adjacent cars would gawk at him. The restaurant he had chosen was full when we got there, but somehow they produced a table. I'm not sure if anyone else in the place ever got their dinner because it seemed like every waiter was circling around our table.

The house had a large Marcy home gym system in the dining room, which Bruce used extensively. The next morning Noriko came across Bruce when he was working out on it. He had her touch his arms and stomach. She still recalls how hard his abdomen was, like chiseled marble.[192]

Later in the day he took us to the movie studio. He had recently filmed the fight scenes for *Game of Death*, including the one with Kareem Abdul-Jabbar. He was fascinated by the opportunity to film a match between two highly-skilled martial artists with such a huge disparity in size. He showed us some of the stills from the footage, which were stunning. He was very happy about the way the scene had turned out, in contrast to a more recent one where he had flown in a well-known martial artist from Korea and had been very disappointed by the caliber of the man's skills. I don't recall him mentioning a name, but presumably it had been Ji Han-Jae.

Bruce shared a story from the filming about how he and Kareem were doing some practice sparring which apparently got a little tense. The fact that a small crowd of movie extras and cameramen were watching—all Chinese—probably ramped up the testosterone level. At any rate, according to Bruce, they were into it. Kareem was using a side kick, his long leg keeping Bruce at bay. Bruce blocked the first kick, and then a second, timing them. Then, on the third kick, he swept it aside and moved in while Kareem's leg was still extended in the air. Sweeping Kareem's remaining leg, Bruce took him down and crouched above him, poised to unleash a series of blows. At which point, again according to Bruce, Kareem threw up his hands saying, "Hey, man, take it easy! We're just sparring." Bruce told the story with his classic giggle.

Bruce also wanted to show us one of the two movies which had been released so far. He selected *The Big Boss*, even though it wasn't as good as *Fist of Fury*, because he thought *Fist of Fury* might offend Noriko. We watched it in a small theater at the studio. I was struck by how late it was in the movie before Bruce appeared, although his presence increased as the film progressed. I didn't realize until much later that Bruce was not originally intended to be the star of the film. Preproduction for the film had already started before Bruce signed his contract with Golden Harvest and showed up in Thailand. Only later during the shooting, after working with Bruce, did Lo Wei decide to kill off the "star" and emphasize Bruce more.[193]

It was obvious to both Noriko and me that Bruce's fame was a mixed blessing. He couldn't go anywhere without attracting a huge crowd. When Dan Inosanto flew in to film the fight for *Game of Death*, it was Linda who picked him up at the airport, to avoid a mob scene.[194]

Offers for various projects were pouring in from Southeast Asian producers and he was being approached by strangers with unclear motives offering checks. According to Linda, he became "totally suspicious of everyone."[195] I don't recall him mentioning the specifics of any of the offers, but Bruce did mention to me that it was hard to know whom to trust. At one point he casually floated the idea of my moving down to Hong Kong when I finished in Tokyo, to help him with his business affairs. We didn't get to the point of discussing the idea at any length, but it was definitely intriguing. On October 24, Noriko and I flew back to Tokyo.

———

WHEN NORIKO AND I were in Hong Kong, I don't recall any mention of a Hollywood deal that was coming together, but one was brewing. Fred Weintraub hadn't given up on a project for Bruce, and pitched a story to Ted Ashley that involved three martial artists (one white, one black and one Chinese) entering a martial arts tournament put on by a criminal boss, titled *Blood and Steel*. Weintraub flew to Hong Kong to negotiate a deal with Raymond Chow in mid-October to co-produce the movie; the negotiations stretched out for a week until Bruce told Chow to make the deal. A few days after Noriko and I flew back to Tokyo, Bruce and Chow flew to Los Angeles to flesh out the details.[196]

The deal did not immediately come together, however. Bruce held out for a number of things that were important to him, and left Los Angeles without a signed contract. Among other things, he wanted the title of the movie changed to *Enter the Dragon*. After some back and forth, he signed a contract in late November, giving him control over all fight choreography, but Warner Bros. was still insisting that the title be *Blood and Steel*.[197]

Way of the Dragon premiered in Hong Kong on December 30, 1972. Within three weeks, by the time filming on *Blood and Steel* had started, it had grossed HK $5.5 million, surpassing *Fist of Fury*'s record and fulfilling Bruce's prediction. But the success was bittersweet. Early in the month, on December 2, Bruce's teacher Yip Man had died. Not knowing of the death, Bruce missed the funeral, for which he received a lot of negative press.[198] And then on December 28 James Lee died, another big blow.[199]

Even before the filming of *Blood and Steel* began in January 1973, initial signs were not overly auspicious. The idea of a co-production in Hong Kong with a Hong Kong studio still seemed like a gamble to Warner Bros. The allotted budget was measly by Hollywood standards, which constrained important decisions at the outset.

One early decision was the director, Bob Clouse, who had scant experience with feature films but was available on the cheap. The same approach was applied for the actors. Martial artist Jim Kelly became the replacement for black actor Rockne Tarkington when the actor quit over low pay on the eve of departure for Hong Kong. Bruce wanted Chuck Norris for the role of one of the major heavies, the criminal boss's bodyguard, but Norris had apparently felt the experience of getting beat up by Bruce in *Way of the Dragon* was enough for him. Bob Wall (also in *Way of the Dragon*) was hired instead. In order to have at least one name actor familiar to American audiences, Weintraub offered the role of the third protagonist to John Saxon, at a pay scale higher than the other actors. He let Saxon think he was going to be the star of the show in order to entice him to accept.[200]

Bruce boycotted the start of the filming over major changes he wanted to the script. Although he viewed the film as his ticket to bigger Hollywood roles, an opportunity he didn't want to blow, he was also extremely concerned about how he would be perceived by Chinese audiences. For instance, rather than play a Chinese James Bond, sent to arrest the evil crime boss on behalf of the British, as the original script called for, Bruce proposed to be a Shaolin monk on a mission to avenge his sister, who had been killed by the crime boss's bodyguard.[201]

Bruce's boycott of the filming lasted for almost two weeks. When he finally returned, problems were not over. On the first day, he got in an argument with Raymond Chow over directorial control and walked off the set.[202]

The first scene Bruce filmed required numerous retakes due to a facial tic he had developed. Fights broke out between extras hired with connections to rival triads. Disputes erupted between the American and Chinese crews. Inferior equipment and electrical malfunctions had to be dealt with. Mishaps such as the capsizing of a boat being towed behind a junk in the movie, a cut from a broken bottle in a fight scene requiring twelve stitches to Bruce's finger, and a bite from a (fortunately) devenomized cobra, further slowed things down. At the same time, Bruce had to contend with challenges from those among the hundreds of extras who wanted their fifteen minutes of fame and figured they had little to lose.[203]

Real prostitutes hired for one scene, because the Chinese actresses refused to play such a role in an American film, demanded compensation in excess of what they would receive for their day job. This in turn caused resentment among the stuntmen, who were being paid far less for more dangerous work.[204]

Tension between the director Bob Clouse and Bruce didn't help, and exacerbated the problems in reconciling ongoing negotiations over script changes. When Bruce discovered that the script writer he thought had been sidelined was still on the job, he blew up, again walking off the set and putting a halt to the filming that was already behind schedule.[205]

The constant stress and physical demands, combined with the oppressive heat and humidity, took their toll. Bruce's weight dropped dramatically, as it had in Thailand during the shoot of *The Big Boss*, and his skin grew "gray and pallid."[206] By the end of the filming he was near exhaustion. Still, after the American crew wrapped up at the beginning of March, he stayed on to perfect the final fight scene in the maze of mirrors, and then an opening scene which establishes his bona fides as a Shaolin monk rather than a British agent.[207]

Tantalizing offers from around the world continued to pour in, including ones from Carlo Ponti to star in a movie with Sophia Loren and from MGM to make a picture with Elvis.[208] As the possibility of a big hit sunk in, Warner Bros. suddenly wanted to sign Bruce up to a multi-picture contract, but Bruce didn't need to jump at offers any more. Toward the end of April he warned Ted Ashley, Warner's president, that he wouldn't come cheap. Stirling Silliphant had also finally gotten approval to make *The Silent Flute*. He enlisted James Coburn to fly to Hong Kong the same month to persuade Bruce to rejoin the project, but Bruce declined to commit.[209]

Bruce was confident *Blood and Steel* would be a big hit. He ordered a customized gold Rolls Royce Corniche from England. But he also hedged his bets again, purchasing some life insurance policies, including one at the very end of April worth multiple millions in today's dollars.[210]

ENDNOTES

177 Polly, *A Life*, pp. 365-366. Originally Bruce wanted to call his directorial debut *Enter the Dragon*, but when a Hollywood opportunity later firmed up, the name was changed to *Way of the Dragon*, so the name would be available for the Hollywood film. Ibid., p. 358.

178 Thomas, *Fighting Spirit*, pp. 147-148; Linda Lee, *The Bruce Lee Story*, p. 125.

179 Linda Lee, *The Bruce Lee Story*, p. 117.

180 Polly, *A Life*, p. 348; Thomas, *Fighting Spirit*, p. 139.

181 Polly, *A Life*, p. 365.

182 Thomas, *Fighting Spirit*, p. 97.

183 Thomas, *Fighting Spirit*, p. 148.

184 Linda Lee, *The Bruce Lee Story*, p. 127; Thomas, *Fighting Spirit*, pp. 148-150. Linda pointed out to me recently that the dialogue in the Hong Kong premier, unlike *The Big Boss* and *Fist of Fury*, was in Cantonese.

185 Thomas, *Fighting Spirit*, pp. 150-151; Polly, *A Life*, p. 374.

186 Polly, *A Life*, p. 370; Linda Lee, *The Bruce Lee Story*, p. 127.

187 Polly, *A Life*, p. 375.

188 Linda Lee, *The Bruce Lee Story*, p. 134; Thomas, *Fighting Spirit*, p. 158.

189 Polly, *A Life*, pp. 382-383; Thomas, *Fighting Spirit*, pp. 158-160.

190 Linda tells me that they did not know James was actually dying of cancer then, only that he was very sick. When he died a couple of months later, it was a shock.

191 In August of 1972 Bruce apparently appeared on Hong Kong's TVB channel as part of a benefit to raise money for victims of a recent typhoon, which may have been the show in question. Thomas, *Fighting Spirit*, p. 222.

192 Noriko was far from the only woman who Bruce asked to feel some part of his musculature. Even his mother was not immune! See Thomas, *Fighting Spirit*, p. 217.

193 Polly, *A Life*, p. 313.

194 Thomas, *Fighting Spirit*, p. 159.

195 Linda Lee, *The Bruce Lee Story*, p. 118.

196 Polly, *A Life*, pp. 404-406; Thomas, *Fighting Spirit*, p. 168. It's not hard to draw the conclusion that Chow was reluctant to do the deal and share his cash cow with Hollywood.

197 Polly, *A Life*, pp. 408. Bruce didn't press the issue at that point, but he had certainly not given up on changing the name.

198 Ibid., pp. 399-400. Apparently none of Yip Man's students or family informed Bruce of the death because he wasn't on good terms with them then.

199 Thomas, *Fighting Spirit*, p. 169.

200 Thomas, *Fighting Spirit*, pp. 171, 176; Polly, *A Life*, pp. 406, 409. Saxon had some background in karate, at one point, according to his Wikipedia bio, taking lessons from Hidetaka Nishiyama, the *karate-ka* whose kicks had impressed Bruce years before when he was in Seattle.

201 Polly, *A Life*, pp. 412-413. In the final version of the movie, he was recruited by the British, but was a Shaolin monk who had his own motive for taking on the job.

202 Linda Lee, *The Bruce Lee Story*, pp. 147-148.

203 Thomas, *Fighting Spirit*, pp. 178-183; Linda Lee, *The Bruce Lee Story*, pp. 136, 140, 148.

204 Polly, *A Life*, p. 418.

205 Thomas, *Fighting Spirit*, p. 175; Polly, *A Life*, pp. 414-415.

206 Thomas, *Fighting Spirit*, p. 180; Polly, *A Life*, p. 423.

207 Polly, *A Life*, pp. 419-420.

208 Linda Lee, *The Man Only I Knew*, p. 177. According to Bob Wall, Bruce was about a month away from signing a contract with Carlo Ponti for a movie to be shot in Rome. Bona, J.J., "Exclusive: Interview with Bob Wall," *Cityonfire.com*, posted January 10, 2011.

209 Polly, *A Life*, pp. 424-425; Thomas, *Fighting Spirit*, p. 192.

210 Thomas, *Fighting Spirit*, p. 188; Polly, *A Life*, p. 425.

CHAPTER 14
An Abrupt End

RELAXATION WAS NOT the default setting for Never Sits Still. He had driven himself relentlessly to finish *Blood and Steel*, and as much as he may have wanted to relax, he found it impossible. He bristled at any suggestion that he do so, pointing out that it was not something one could will himself to do. He may also have convinced himself that he was relaxing while working.[211]

If there was any doubt that he was driving himself too hard, the question should have been settled on May 10, 1973, when he had his first seizure. Bruce was in a dubbing room at Golden Harvest, looping dialogue for *Blood and Steel* in a tiny sweltering room. The air conditioning had been turned off so the noise wouldn't interfere with the recording. Bruce said he felt faint and excused himself to go to the restroom. When he was found on the floor after a long absence, he pretended he was looking for his contacts. After being helped back to the dubbing room, he collapsed again, vomiting and having trouble breathing.[212]

He was rushed to the hospital, where he had to be held down and taped to control his seizure-like convulsions. The doctors deduced cerebral edema (swelling of the brain) and administered a drug to reduce it; they were ready to perform brain surgery if the drug didn't work.[213]

Fortunately the drug worked, and after a couple of hours Bruce showed signs of recovery. When he was able to speak, he told Linda that he had felt "very close to death."

OVER THE NEXT few days, the doctors tried to determine the cause of the cerebral edema. When Bruce told one of the doctors that he had eaten a little hash, the doctor suggested that might have caused the collapse. Bruce took exception to the suggestion and refused further tests, saying he would get some in the States.[214]

Linda confirms that Bruce used cannabis on occasion, which he thought made him more creative. He probably also used it to relax. Although he has been made out to sound like a stoner in some accounts, there is no way he could have worked so hard and so long and accomplished what he did if he was high all the time. He was also very health conscious—drinking high protein drinks and his own concoctions of blended fruits and vegetables and taking multiple vitamins.[215] He didn't believe that cannabis was a health concern.

Two weeks after the collapse, Bruce and Linda flew to Los Angeles for a second opinion. After extensive tests, the Los Angeles doctors were stumped. They observed that he was in superb condition and gave him a clean bill of health. They ruled out cannabis as the culprit. As a precaution, they prescribed Dilantin (phenytoin, an anticonvulsant).[216] But to friends who knew him, he wasn't the same Bruce. According to Bob Wall, he looked "chalky white and thin, nervous and upset;" he seemed "jumbled, unsure, and just plain worn out. . . [and occasionally] would repeat himself in conversation."[217]

While they were in Los Angeles, the studio had an early screening of *Blood and Steel*. The film was not yet finished—the music soundtrack and other effects were still to be added—but everyone who watched it knew they had a winner. A date in August was set for the premier and Bruce agreed to return to the States then to help promote the film, including an appearance on *The Johnny Carson Show*.[218]

Bruce felt his opportunities had expanded exponentially. He felt confident enough to turn down the revived *Silent Flute*. He called Stirling Silliphant to tell Silliphant that he couldn't afford him—that he was being offered a million dollars a picture.[219]

In early June, Bruce and Linda returned to Hong Kong. Soon thereafter, he was finally able to persuade Warners to change the name *Blood and Steel* to *Enter the Dragon*. Warners resisted, proposing *Han's Island* as an alternative. But Bruce held firm. At that point Warners wanted to sign Bruce for follow-up films and beat a strategic retreat. On June 13, 1973, Ted Ashley sent Bruce a telegram confirming that the name would be *Enter the Dragon*.[220] Bruce was elated.

The economic reality, however, was that Bruce and Linda were still far from out of the financial woods. *Enter the Dragon* was not yet released. They were living off advances against anticipated earnings from *Way of the Dragon*, but Bruce's share of the profits was just trickling in. He suspected he was being cheated by Raymond Chow.[221]

Other pressures had also not decreased. Despite his collapse, and the fact that even he attributed it to "overwork and stress,"[222] he was unable to slow down. Each time he met one goal, he replaced it with another. In the view of John Saxon, his life was "spiraling away."[223] At the same time, living in Hong Kong was even more like living in a fishbowl. He couldn't go out without a crowd gathering, and everything he did received critical press attention.[224] At some point he decided to move back to the States, perhaps returning to Hong Kong a couple of times a year to pursue specialized film projects.[225]

And then there were the mood swings. One minute he would assert that there was "no limit, no end in sight" to what he could achieve; the next, he would confess to Linda that he didn't know how much longer he could "keep this up."[226]

An uncharacteristic incident with Lo Wei illustrates the effect the stress was having on his state of mind. On July 10, 1973, Bruce was in the Golden Harvest studios and heard that the director Lo Wei and his wife were in a screening room elsewhere on the premises. Lo Wei had been quoted in the press making critical comments about Bruce and taking credit for his success. Bruce decided to confront Lo Wei and a raucous argument ensued.

After they were separated, Bruce returned to Raymond Chow's office. Lo Wei's wife followed to chastise Bruce for his lack of decorum. Bruce blew up again and raced back to the screening room. He pulled out a short knife he wore hidden in his belt buckle and brandished it. Lo Wei called the police to complain that Bruce had threatened him. When the police arrived, they were unable to find the knife and belt buckle, but pressured Bruce to write a statement promising to leave Lo Wei alone.[227] Linda confirms that Bruce pulled his belt buckle knife during the confrontation. In her words, it "wasn't his finest hour."

That night Bruce appeared on a TV show. When asked, he denied the claim that he had pulled a knife on Lo Wei, arguing that if he had wanted to harm Lo Wei his hands would have been enough. In support of his argument, he demonstrated a pre-rehearsed push to the TV host's shoulder that sent him flying. The demonstration backfired, and the morning newspapers portrayed Bruce as a bully.[228]

Bruce had always had a quick temper, but in his later years had kept it under control. Indeed, he went out of his way to avoid actual fisticuffs. When he did end up in a fight, he used the minimum amount of force needed to bring it to an end. He collected weapons and books on weapons, and he had had several belt buckle knives made for himself, thinking (in Linda's words) that they were rather "clever." But to my knowledge (and Linda's), he had never before threatened anyone with a weapon. He certainly didn't need one with Lo Wei, an older man with no particular martial arts skills. The fact that he pulled one during the encounter was a huge flashing neon sign that something was akilter.

The claim has been made that Bruce also began carrying a gun in Hong Kong. I seriously doubt that claim, however. For one thing, guns (in contrast to knives) were rare in Hong Kong, and carrying one entailed serious legal consequences. Linda emphatically denies that he ever carried one.[229]

Another claim is that as he became more isolated in his last months he ingested increasing amounts of hash and drank more and more sake.[230] I can't speak to the hash. As to the alcohol, his body did not react well to it; I never saw him take more than a sip. Supposedly he developed a tolerance for sake,[231] but it seems strange to me that of all the various alcoholic beverages he would only be able to tolerate sake. Although she acknowledges that he consumed cannabis, Linda denies that he drank. Since he was still suffering from chronic back pain, with all the other pressures during that period it is imaginable that he might have begun to self-medicate with alcohol as well as cannabis in addition to the Darvon he took. But if he was, it was another indication that things were awry.

It does seem clear that in his final months Bruce's mood swings were growing more pronounced and that his friends believed his behavior was more erratic. As one example, a childhood friend who was in the film business recounted that Bruce called him a few days before his death when he was on location in Manila. In a rambling phone call, Bruce apparently complained of headaches he was having.[232] Jesse also recounts that Jhoon Rhee visited Bruce in Hong Kong a few months before his death and told Taky that Bruce "wasn't the same person he had previously been;" that he was "nervous, suspicious, and difficult to get along with."[233]

———

ON JULY 20, 1973 it all came to a head. There are different perspectives as to the exact details and sequence of events, but the facts that matter seem clear. Bruce had started working again on *Game of Death*, and in the late afternoon or early evening he and Raymond Chow were at the apartment of an actress who was to have a leading role in the film, Betty Ting Pei. Bruce complained of a headache, and Raymond left to prepare for a dinner that Bruce and Betty were also to attend. Betty gave Bruce a tablet of Equagesic (a tranquilizer), which a doctor had prescribed for her, and he lay down to rest.[234]

When Raymond Chow later called to see why they were late for the dinner, Betty Ting Pei was unable to wake Bruce up. By the time Raymond returned to her apartment and they called a doctor, who summoned an ambulance, hours had gone by. Some of the symptoms were reminiscent of the collapse two months before. But this time Bruce never recovered.[235]

The location of Bruce's fatal collapse was initially not reported accurately. When the Hong Kong newspapers found out the actual location, they went wild. Others have written about Bruce's alleged affairs and relationship with Betty Ting Pei. I don't know about that. It has nothing to do with all of Bruce's accomplishments. What I do know is that Bruce loved Linda, Brandon and Shannon; and when he played with his kids, he was a different person.[236] Linda was Bruce's confidant, sounding board, and a calming influence. Without her yin to his yang, I doubt he would have achieved all that he did.

An autopsy was conducted several days after Bruce's death. The funeral in Hong Kong held two days after that was a circus, with over 15,000 people gathered for a glimpse of the casket. The following day his body was flown to Seattle for a more sedate ceremony.[237] He was buried there in Lake View Cemetery in the Capitol Hill neighborhood, not far from the house Linda grew up in.

I WAS STILL in Tokyo. When I first heard of Bruce's death, from another American lawyer in the office who had heard the news on a U.S. armed forces radio station, I was gobsmacked. The first thing that entered my mind was the story he told when I was in Hong Kong nine months before, about his encounter with the master of internal *qi* on the Hong Kong TV show in front of an audience of millions. The master had no doubt lost a lot of face. I wondered if Bruce had been poisoned.

Noriko and I were not able to attend either of the funerals from Tokyo. My parents attended the one in Seattle, which my mother described in a letter. They were impressed by Linda's composure and fortitude in appearing and sharing her thoughts with those in attendance. My mother was also impressed with Taky's appearance, at the beginning and end of his remarks giving Bruce's *gung fu* salutation facing the casket and an enlarged photo of Bruce placed above it.[238]

Linda wrote a gracious note to my parents after the funeral, thanking them for the flowers they had sent. The card had a quote from Kahlil Gibran: "If someone tells you the soul perishes like the body and that which dies never returns, tell him the flower perishes but the seed remains and lies before us as the secret of life everlasting." After the inscription she wrote:

Dear Mr. and Mrs. Palmer,

Bruce always felt he had a special friendship with you and your sons. I am glad that you were able to know and appreciate Bruce though his years were short. I know Bruce would want to thank you for being kind enough to take him into your family for a time. Thank you for caring.

Love, Linda

Bruce and I had kept in loose touch after we re-connected, and I had been seriously entertaining the idea of moving down to Hong Kong to work for Bruce when my contract ended at the end of the summer. His sudden death of course put an end to that possibility. With no other plan in mind, I extended my contract in Tokyo for an additional six months.

———

A MONTH AFTER Bruce's death, in August of 1973, *Enter the Dragon* premiered at Grauman's Chinese Theater in Los Angeles. The premier was a spectacle, with lion dancers in the streets and overflow crowds. Linda attended, but it was hard for her with the shock of Bruce's death so fresh in her mind, watching the raw power of his performance on the screen without him sitting next to her.[239]

Everyone had expected *Enter the Dragon* to be a hit. It had gone way over budget, but when the first cut was viewed, Warner Bros. appropriated an extra $50,000 for special music and sound effects.[240] But the rapidity and extent of its success took everyone by surprise. By the end of the year it had grossed $90 million world-wide.[241]

Although he too thought it would be a hit, Bruce had also been very apprehensive. He had put everything on the line, but was concerned whether an Asian actor would be accepted in the West, and whether Chinese audiences would think the movie was too Western.[242] He needn't have worried. Although it did not do as well in Hong Kong as his previous films, it was still a hit there; and its success across the rest of the world more than made up for it. Unfortunately, Bruce did not live to see his wildest dreams come true and watch his fame surpass his friends and rivals James Coburn and Steve McQueen.

―――――――

ALL MANNER OF rumors regarding the cause of Bruce's death circulated in the weeks following. The fact that the autopsy had found cannabis in Bruce's stomach (along with Equagesic) further inflamed the rumors. In some quarters Betty Ting Pei was blamed, and a bomb threat was even called in to the police. To calm things down, the British colonial government ordered an inquest.[243]

The inquest took place from September 3 to September 24. A multitude of witnesses were called to testify, including Linda and Raymond Chow and Betty Ting Pei as well as the doctors who pronounced him dead and other medical experts. Lawyers for the insurance companies which had insured Bruce's life earlier in the year questioned some of the witnesses in an effort to establish cannabis as the cause of death, since that would have provided grounds for a denial of the insurance proceeds.[244]

The cannabis theory was effectively debunked at the inquest. In its place, Equagesic was touted as the probable cause, with its aspirin or meprobamate, or the combination, proposedly causing an allergic reaction that led to the cerebral edema. But according to Betty Ting Pei, Bruce had taken Equagesic before without any reaction.[245] Moreover, he hadn't taken Equagesic before his prior collapse, which had some of the same symptoms.[246]

Despite my initial thought when I heard the news of his death, I don't think Bruce was poisoned, or the victim of a furtive application of a *dim mak* delayed death touch technique.[247] Perhaps if his fatal collapse had been the only one of its kind, the possibility would be worth more consideration. But with the previous collapse two months before his death, some natural cause seems more likely.

Polly's recent book has come up with a new theory that blames heatstroke. He makes a plausible case. Jesse Glover has written about Bruce's susceptibility to heat, noting that his control deteriorated when it was hot.[248] It was definitely hot and muggy on the days of both of his collapses. And Bruce did have an operation to remove the sweat glands underneath his arm pits a short while before his first collapse, which would have exacerbated his vulnerability to heat. But Bruce grew up in Hong Kong, and had been back for a couple of years. He was no stranger to such conditions. In addition, his other uncharacteristic behavior in the months before his death suggests to me that something else was going on.

Linda confirms that Bruce had been taking Darvon to alleviate his chronic back pain.[249] Darvon and generic propoxyphene were banned by the FDA in 2010, but Darvon was available over the counter then in Hong Kong and Bruce had used it frequently over an extended period of time. She speculates that the Darvon may have had a long-term effect on Bruce's body. Darvon was apparently banned by the FDA because of deaths resulting from heart problems, but the online information on the drug lists potential adverse effects which include abnormal behavior, coma, vomiting and convulsions.[250] Linda mentioned the possibility more as a conjecture than a belief, but Bruce's aberrant behavior in the months before his death makes it a plausible one. The Dilantin he was taking as an anticonvulsant also sometimes interacts negatively with pain narcotics like Darvon.

The bottom line, however, is that after an autopsy, inquest and endless speculation over the ensuing decades, the cause of the cerebral edema that led to his death remains a mystery.

—————

AFTER FINISHING UP in Tokyo in early 1974, Noriko and I moved back to Seattle. Taky still ran Bruce's school there. He had an IGA store on 8th and Madison on First Hill, and had cleared out part of the basement for the class, next to a storage area. I rejoined the class soon after I returned.

Taky had turned over most of the day to day oversight of the class to an assistant instructor, an ex-British commando who had once boxed professionally and was big on physical conditioning. I was okay with all the sit-ups and push-ups, and loved putting on the gloves and climbing into the ring set up in a corner of the basement once in a while, but the class wasn't the same.

The class faithfully preserved Bruce's techniques, as modified from the original Seattle days, and we sparred a lot. But it was the same limited set of techniques practiced over and over. Even that was alright up to a point—they were highly effective techniques. The problem was, I felt no sense of an expanding, evolving open-ended system. The excitement of discovery was missing. There was no Bruce. I kept at it for a number of years for the physical conditioning, but eventually dropped out.

Fortunately, I never had the occasion to seriously need to use any of the techniques, but the training still came in handy.

One night I was walking after work along First Avenue, then still considered to be Seattle's Skid Road, with block after block of cheap bars and peep shows.[251] I was headed to the 211 Club, a classic pool hall just off First, to meet up with Toshi Moriguchi (the old high school friend whom I had threatened to borrow money from when I was invited to stay with Bruce's family in Hong Kong two decades before). Toshi was still shooting pool on a regular basis.

As I walked along First Avenue, I noticed some sort of disturbance in front of a bar on the other side of the street. Suddenly a man who looked to be Native American raced through traffic across the street, narrowly avoiding a car. A younger man was in hot pursuit. The younger man caught up with him a little ways in front of me, knocking him to the ground, then proceeding to kick him. The older man curled up in a ball to try to weather the kicks.

I didn't know what had transpired between the two, or who was the original aggressor, but the guy lying on the ground wasn't any kind of threat. I stepped up, close enough to be heard and intervene if necessary, but not within kicking range. I told the younger man to knock it off.

The man turned from the guy on the ground, who quickly regained his feet and ran off while his attacker's attention was otherwise occupied. The man was clearly angry, and his ire was now directed at me. I stood there a few paces away, my right side turned slightly toward him, in a position Bruce had taught us for being prepared without signaling aggressive intent. I was acutely aware that I was wearing my glasses.

The man swore at me and told me to mind my own business, then contemplated his next move. I waited, right elbow cupped in my left hand, the right forearm vertical in front of me, ready to move instantly as my right thumb and forefinger seemingly absently scratched my chin and nose.

After a few seconds the man swore again. "You're lucky you're wearing glasses," he said. I shrugged, realizing he had decided not to press the matter, which was fine by me. Mission accomplished.

ENDNOTES

211 Linda Lee, *The Bruce Lee Story*, p. 155.

212 Ibid., pp. 151-152.

213 Ibid., p. 153.

214 Polly, *A Life*, pp. 427-428. Authorities in Hong Kong, including medical authorities, viewed cannabis then with even more suspicion than it was viewed in the States. Linda recalls one of the doctors as being a devout Baptist. Neither of them had any medical experience with cannabis.

215 Linda Lee, *The Bruce Lee Story*, p. 144.

216 Thomas, *Fighting Spirit*, pp. 190-191; Polly, *A Life*, pp. 428, 461.

217 Thomas, *Fighting Spirit*, p. 191. My daughter and son-in-law, both medical doctors, commented that these symptoms sound consistent with narcotic withdrawal. Since Bruce was still taking the opioid Darvon for his back pain, but apparently only when he needed it, it is conceivable that he had withdrawal symptoms but then took Darvon again when the pain flared up, thus perpetuating a vicious cycle. This was at a time long before the current opioid crisis familiarized people with the dangers of prescription drugs.

218 Thomas, *Fighting Spirit*, pp. 191-192; Linda Lee, *The Bruce Lee Story*, p. 154.

219 Polly, *A Life*, p. 432.

220 Polly, *A Life*, pp. 420-421. See Linda Lee, *The Bruce Lee Story*, p. 133, for a copy of the telegram.

221 Thomas, *Fighting Spirit*, p. 193.

222 Polly, *A Life*, p. 431.

223 Linda Lee, *The Bruce Lee Story*, p. 155.

224 Among other things, the coverage questioned how "Chinese" he really was and sniped about his relationship with his teacher Yip Man and the Wing Chun school. Polly, *A Life*, pp. 391, 397.

225 Linda Lee, *The Bruce Lee Story*, p. 154.

226 Ibid., p. 155.

227 Polly, *A Life*, pp. 434-435; Thomas, *Fighting Spirit*, pp. 193-194.

228 Polly, *A Life*, p. 436; Thomas, *Fighting Spirit*, p. 194.

229 Polly, *A Life*, in the notes to p. 389, cites *Bruce Lee: King of Kung-fu*, a book by Felix Dennis and Don Atyeo, p. 67, for that claim. Dennis and Atyeo do not provide any source for it. I have never heard or read of this anywhere else. Furthermore, the anecdote recounted by Dennis and Atyeo which is the basis for the claim does not ring true for other reasons. The anecdote is that when Bruce went to his old high school to present awards for a Sports Day, he introduced Bob Baker as his "bodyguard" and later told the principal that he had a gun inside a bag he was carrying. But the Sports Day he attended was in February of 1973, during the filming of *Enter the Dragon*. Bob Baker was not in that film, and according to Linda not in Hong Kong then. It would also seem to defeat the purpose to carry a gun around in a bag.

230 Thomas, *Fighting Spirit*, p. 198; Polly, *A Life*, p. 430.

231 Polly, *A Life*, p. 424.

232 Thomas, *Fighting Spirit*, pp. 198-200.

233 Glover, *Bruce Lee*, p. 90.

234 See Linda Lee, *The Bruce Lee Story*, p. 157, and Polly, *A Life*, pp. 439-441. Equagesic is a combination of aspirin and meprobamate. In that combination, meprobamate is used as a muscle relaxant, but it apparently also can have some serious side effects, including life-threatening allergic reactions. See, e.g., www.rxlist.com/meprobamate-side-effects-drug-center.htm#overview.

235 Linda Lee, *The Bruce Lee Story*, pp. 157-158; Polly, *A Life*, pp. 441-443.

236 According to Fred Weintraub, the only time he thought he saw the real Bruce toward the end was when he was playing with his kids. Linda Lee, *The Bruce Lee Story*, p. 149.

237 Polly, *A Life*, pp. 1-5.

238 Steve McQueen and James Coburn flew up to Seattle to act as pallbearers (along with brother Robert, Taky, Dan Inosanto and Peter Chin, a family friend from Los Angeles), and Coburn gave a short graveside farewell. Thomas, *Fighting Spirit*, p. 207. My mother didn't mention either of them in her letter.

239 Linda Lee, *The Bruce Lee Story*, pp. 185, 188.

240 Linda Lee, *The Bruce Lee Story*, p. 149.

241 Polly, *A Life*, p. 478.

242 Linda Lee, *The Bruce Lee Story*, pp. 146-147.

243 Polly, *A Life*, p. 453.

244 Ibid., pp. 456-472.

245 Ibid., p. 441.

246 The closeness in time of the two collapses, and the fact that Bruce never suffered such a collapse before, make it hard not to draw the conclusion that they were related. But although both resulted in cerebral edema, there is no evidence that he had any convulsions during his second collapse.

247 These were only two of the rumors that circulated after his death. Some of the screwier ones were that he was assassinated by Japanese *ninja*, hacked to death by young thugs, and died from too much sex. Polly, *A Life*, pp. 450-451.

248 Glover, *Bruce Lee*, p. 71.

249 At the inquest, Linda testified that Bruce had taken Doloxene for his back pain. Polly, *A Life*, p. 461. Doloxene may only have contained propoxyphene as the active ingredient. The inquest apparently overlooked Darvon (or Doloxene) entirely as a possible cause.

250 Ironically, the online information also includes headaches—the reason Betty Ting Pei gave Bruce the tablet of Equagesic—as a possible side effect.

251 The original Skid Road in Seattle is now Yesler Way, where logs were literally skidded down the hill to a sawmill at the bottom, located near where First Avenue intersects.

Author and Muhammad Ali, Beijing, 1993

CHAPTER 15
Bruce and Muhammad Ali

T HE SECOND OCCASION I met Muhammad Ali was on a trip to Beijing in 1993, when China was competing for the 2000 Olympics. In order to show the world it could put on a world-class sporting event, China decided to stage its first professional fight card, *The Brawl at the Wall*. As it turned out, the Chinese company sponsoring the fights was scammed out of several million dollars by a couple of Seattle boxing promoters, who presented phony contracts with name boxers; the law firm I then worked for in Seattle was retained to help recover the money. The Chinese company also had to scramble to line up a real fight card on short notice when the phony card fell through, with which I helped out. Ali himself was no longer fighting, but he was revered in China and was invited by the Chinese as a special guest to appear for the event.

Another lawyer and I were invited along to attend the event. The Chinese sponsor chartered a Boeing 747 to ferry all the fighters and their trainers and handlers from San Francisco to Beijing. We were seated on the top deck, along with Ali and others. Then showing symptoms of Parkinson's, Ali walked and spoke tentatively, but his physical presence and charisma were still awesome. And there were numerous instances during the trip where he demonstrated that the parallels between him and Bruce were many.

On the plane over, he entertained the flight attendants with various stunts, including his ability to "levitate." With the stewardesses several paces in front of him, his feet quivered and appeared to slowly rise an inch or so off the deck. From my vantage point behind him, it was apparent his heels were still firmly grounded while the front half of his feet were lifted up seemingly parallel to the deck. The stewardesses were vastly amused.

The plane landed in Shanghai in the middle of the night to clear immigration, before continuing on to Beijing. The passengers all stumbled groggily off the plane and up a gangway toward the immigration area. I was right behind Ali, and noticed a number of blinding bright lights at the far end of the gangway. As we neared, it became clear that the lights were accompanying members of the Chinese news media with TV cameras, who had somehow gained access to the immigration area. A reporter shoved a microphone in front of Ali and asked in English, "Do you like China?"

Ali halted, seemingly dazed by the lights and lack of sleep. Then he looked straight at the camera. "No, I don't like China," he said, pausing a beat. "I *love* China." He was asked several more questions, but those first lines dominated all of the TV news programs the following day in Beijing.

If Ali was with us, everywhere we went in Beijing was in a long motorcade with a platoon of motorcycle cops leapfrogging ahead to stop traffic. At one venue Ali was surrounded by a crowd of uniformed soldiers who were gawking or asking for his autograph. Over their heads Ali spotted a group of kids, none of whom could get near because of the crowd. Ali slowly pushed his way through the soldiers over to the kids and passed out small copies of his photograph.

I CONFESS THAT I sometimes wondered—perhaps like many folks—how Bruce would have fared if he had been matched against Ali.

One might think that the two were in different classes—at 6'-3" and over 210 pounds (he was listed as 226 pounds when he fought Mac Foster), Ali was a true heavyweight; at 5'-8" and around 135 or 140 pounds, Bruce was a lightweight or welterweight. Bruce himself often said that a "good big man would beat a good small man." All other things being equal, size mattered. And some things in my view were equal between the two of them.

They both worked hard to perfect their skills, had a very competitive nature and a lot of grit. Ali raced the school bus to train in high school; Bruce was a perfectionist who practiced constantly to hone his physical abilities and technique. And they both had the consummate fighter's sense of distance. Both were able to judge how far an opponent's arms or legs could reach and stay at the edge of or outside that range until they closed the gap. Ali is said to have divided the ring mentally into "safety zones," which he would hover at the edge of with his hands by his sides. Bruce too had an uncanny ability in that regard.

But that wasn't the end of the story. Indeed, not all things besides size *were* equal. Bruce had some things going for him that might have tipped the scales in his favor.

One factor was speed—not just hand speed, but reflexes. Needless to say, Ali had both hand speed and reflexes in abundance. I still have a vision of his controversial fight against Ernie Terrell in February of 1967. Terrell had refused to call him Muhammad

Ali, the name he adopted to replace his "slave name," Cassius Clay. Ali apparently took it personally.

The controversy arose from the fact that Ali was portrayed by some sportswriters as needlessly taunting Terrell. During the fight, after six rounds of dancing around Terrell and giving him a boxing lesson, Ali repeatedly dropped both hands and thrust his head forward as he approached Terrell shouting, "What's my name?" Terrell threw a number of punches, all of which Ali avoided by mere millimeters, leaning back slightly or shifting his head from side to side without using his hands to block. In doing that, he certainly demonstrated his sense of distance. But awesome reflexes were also needed. Terrell was humiliated, although he showed his own brand of grit by going the whole fifteen rounds without being knocked down.

No question, Ali was unusually fast, and not just for a heavyweight. He reputedly had a faster jab than even Sugar Ray Robinson, the welterweight/middleweight who is sometimes called the greatest boxer ever, pound for pound. But as fast as Ali was, I believe that Bruce was faster. Being smaller, it would make sense that he would be. I'm not aware of any definitive scientific comparison of the two, but when Bruce was filming fight scenes, he had to slow his movements down because otherwise they showed up just as a blur. He also personified the old saw that "the hand is quicker than the eye."

One of his favorite parlor tricks was to place a dime in someone's upturned palm and then take a couple of steps back. "I'm going to snatch the coin out of your hand," he would say. "See if you can close your hand before I do." He would make sure the person was ready, then dart forward in a blur and step back again. Inevitably the person would stand there with his hand clenched, a grim smile on his face, certain the coin was still safely wrapped inside his fist. The look of incredulity when he opened his hand to find it empty, as Bruce flourished the coin from several feet away, was always priceless.

To rub salt in the wound, Bruce would sometimes offer to give the person another try. This time the person was absolutely sure the coin was still there—he or she could definitely feel it. The person would triumphantly open his or her hand, only to gape even more incredulously at the penny which had replaced the dime.

Of course, speed doesn't necessarily trump size. The impact of a fist depends on its mass (weight) as well as its speed. So a person with a larger fist (and body behind it) might be able to deliver a blow with more impact, even though the punch was slower. But here too, Bruce more than compensated for his smaller size. Just as a roundhouse haymaker thrown with just the arm isn't as powerful as a punch with the shoulders and torso behind it, Bruce was able to literally harness his whole body behind a punch. He could channel the force of his entire body weight through his arm to the end of his fist. Anyone who has seen his one-inch punch, with which he could send a much larger man who was bracing himself flying on his ass, knows the force he could generate.

In addition to reflexes and hand speed, speed at closing the gap is also important. Ali was no slouch in that department, but Bruce— perhaps because he often had to deal with larger opponents—was a master. The snatched coin trick, where he often started several steps away from the hand holding the coin, demonstrated that. But he especially loved the challenge of putting that skill into practice by sparring with much bigger men, like with Kareem Abdul-Jabbar.

One of the points that I took away from the story he told about his sparring with Kareem on the *Game of Death* movie set, where he had to time Kareem's kick's precisely, was that size indeed did matter. If Bruce had been sparring with me, for instance, a mere

6'-2", he would not have had to time several of my kicks before moving in. He would have been there on the first kick. Ali was a lot bigger than Bruce, but nowhere near as big as Kareem. And what if Bruce was fighting an opponent who didn't kick?

Which leads to the fourth factor that might have evened the playing field in any encounter between Bruce and Ali—the fact that they came from very different disciplines. By its very nature, boxing has a set of rules which circumscribes the tools that can be used—only fists for striking (no feet, knees, elbows or head butts), and punches directed only at specific areas (no blows below the belt or to the back of the head). The gloves also greatly limit the type of blows (e.g., no finger jabs to the eyes, and it's hard to effectively hit the throat with gloves on). Of course, boxers cheat in the ring; my boxing coach, Walter Michael, knew all the tricks (eye gouging with the thumb of the glove, using the laces on the glove to scrape the skin raw with a glancing punch, placing the feet to trip the opponent when moving in close in a judo-like maneuver that was hard for the ref to spot, to name just a few). But even the dirty tricks in boxing are limited in scope.

Bruce's approach to fighting brooked no rules. In the few real matches he is known for, he insisted that they be "no holds barred." He may have insisted on that more for the principle—when the matches actually occurred he never did anything that maimed or seriously injured his opponent. (As mentioned earlier, I don't believe he tried to jab Wong Jack Man in the eyes with his fingers.)

But the point is, boxing is inherently more restricted in its repertoire than Bruce's Jeet Kune Do. And while a boxer can certainly train to defend against techniques from another discipline, there is only so much one can train in a limited amount of time against a practitioner who has been steeped in that discipline for his entire fighting career. The ill-conceived match between Muhammad Ali and Antonio Inoki, which took place in Japan in June of 1976, is a case in point.[252]

The fight went fifteen rounds and ended in a draw, with Inoki on his back throughout the fight, trying to trip or kick Ali, and Ali circling him. Apparently Ali only threw a few punches during the whole fight, not surprising given that Inoki was on his back most of the time. But the bizarre nature of the fight was effectively pre-ordained by the very rules that were established beforehand— no leg-dives or tackles, no kicking unless one knee was on the mat. Even so, according to one report Ali sustained blood clots in his leg from the kicks that almost resulted in his leg being amputated later.[253] Although the fight may have been a pre-cursor to modern mixed martial arts, it was not a good example of it. There are apparently different claims about how the rules for the fight came to be implemented, but it isn't hard to imagine that Ali's camp must have thought it important to have them. One can only wonder how the match would have gone if there hadn't been any.

Likewise, one can only wonder how Bruce and Ali would have fared against each other. Bruce unquestionably learned a lot from watching Ali's fight films and mimicking Ali's balletic moves. But Ali learned from Bruce, too, through their mutual friend, Jhoon Rhee, who taught Ali what he called the "Accupunch" (a way of punching without telegraphing, which Bruce had taught to Rhee). According to Rhee, Ali used the punch in his *Thrilla in Manila* fight against Frazier in 1975, and then later in knock-down blows against the English and European heavyweight champion Richard Dunn in May of 1976.[254] Jhoon Rhee was also part of Ali's entourage for the Inoki farce.[255]

Another important factor in any physical confrontation is the shape that the fighters are in. Ali, when he fought in his prime, was obviously in top physical condition—he had to be to go fifteen grueling rounds of constant movement while absorbing brutal punishment. Bruce did not get seriously into conditioning until after his encounter with Wong Jack Man, but as with all things he did, once he got into it, he really got into it. A related factor is how well the fighter can take a punch. We know that Ali could take one, especially after his fights with Frazier. With Bruce, we can only assume that he could, given all the street fights he had as a kid before he became a great martial artist. So as to these factors, I would rate them roughly even (although, due to his greater size, perhaps Ali could have taken a greater punch).

Jhoon Rhee says that Bruce was pessimistic about his chances against Ali, noting the small size of his hand as compared to Ali's.[256] But Bruce was not a braggart, and was always diplomatic when asked to compare his ability to someone else's, even when in his heart he was probably confident he could prevail. And Bruce knew better than anyone that the size of one's hand was not the determining factor in a no-holds-barred fight.

Of course, we'll never know. Even if they were both still around, an encounter between them would be best left in the imagination. For all the reasons listed above, I think Bruce would have more than held his own. But regardless of the outcome, it would in no way have diminished the enduring legacies that both Bruce and Ali have left us. In my mind, they will always remain among The Greatest.

ENDNOTES

252 The Ali/Inoki fight was reffed by Gene LeBell, a former pro wrestler and stuntman who worked with Bruce on the *Green Hornet* set, and who taught Bruce some grappling techniques. Linda Lee, *The Bruce Lee Story*, p. 175.

253 Aaron Tallent (February 20, 2005). "The Joke That Almost Ended Ali's Career." *The Sweet Science*.

254 Jhoon Rhee, *Bruce Lee and I*, p. 132.

255 Josh Gross (June 21, 2016). "Ali vs. Inoki: The Forgotten Fight That Inspired Mixed Martial Arts and Launched Sports Entertainment." *BenBella Books*. ISBN 978-1-942-95219-0.

256 Bruce told him, "Look at my hand. That's a little Chinese hand. He'd kill me." Jhoon Rhee, *Bruce Lee and I*, p. 131.

Author in *bai jong*, Hong Kong, summer 1963

CHAPTER 16

Legacy

BRUCE WAS EVOLVING and expanding his conceptual framework and skills his entire life. He was able to do so for several reasons—his natural abilities allowed it, his temperament compelled him, and circumstances laid a strong foundation and a path for him to expand his horizons.

The natural abilities we assume Bruce was born with were not evident early in his life. He was a sickly child who remained a skinny kid and was often picked on when he started school. He undoubtedly received his share of lumps from the encounters. Obviously his unimposing physique masked a tremendous potential. But it was his temperament which compelled him to develop his average-sized frame to the absolute limits of possibility.

Even as a skinny child, he was gutsy; he fought back when he was picked on. As he grew older, he pushed himself. Men up to a decade or more older, with years of judo or boxing under their belt, were drawn to him. Bruce in turn loved to gather other martial artists around him. He loved to test himself physically against them, and his evolving Wing Chun techniques against their skills. This did not change in later years, even as his reputation as a martial artist grew. In his movies, he made it a point to cast people who were martial artists first, rather than actors who may have had some martial arts training.

He was lackadaisical if he wasn't interested in something, but intense and disciplined if he was. When he did incorporate techniques he ran across, his natural ability and the hours he practiced on his own made the additions seamless, like integral branches on an already sturdy trunk. He never hesitated to incorporate techniques into his own repertoire if they worked. Yet despite his natural physical abilities and innate drive to develop them, it was external circumstances when he was growing up which allowed them to develop fully.

The crowded streets of Hong Kong and their rich ferment, with gangs and rivalries and the constant goad of being part of a Chinese majority under the heavy thumb of the British, with the subtext of being of mixed heritage, were a constant stimulant. In addition, a *gung fu* school in the form of Yip Man's Wing Chun, with its emphasis on practical results, and Yip Man's willingness to take Bruce under his wing, was there when he needed it. But perhaps most important, the fact that he was born in San Francisco as a U.S. citizen allowed him the opportunity to strike out on his own when he was ready for a broader platform.

If he had stayed in Hong Kong, it is likely he would have developed into one of the top Wing Chun practitioners. But he would probably not have been exposed to the array of martial arts experts from such a wide variety of backgrounds and abilities that opened him up to the endless possibilities of the world, and sparked his own evolution as a martial artist and a human being.[257] It was all encapsulated there in the name his parents gave him—Jun Fan, or "Shaking Up San Francisco."

THE DEMANDS ON Bruce and the struggle to control his own destiny did not end when he died. Indeed, although time has smoothed out some of the currents his death set in motion, some eddies still ripple today.

Bruce's first major post-mortem battle was with the insurance companies that tried to weasel out of paying off his life insurance policies. His cannabis usage was focused on during the inquest because it offered the insurance companies a means of denying coverage. Ultimately the insurance companies settled for a portion of the policy amounts.

Meanwhile, neither Linda nor the estate had any other ready source of funds. Bruce had little cash or tangible assets when he died. Golden Harvest owned the rights to the two movies he had made for it. The rights to his third movie (*Way of the Dragon*) were owned by Concord Productions, the joint venture owned 50/50 by Bruce and Raymond Chow. The rights to *Enter the Dragon*, Bruce's fourth and last film, were shared by Warner Bros. and Concord. But Raymond Chow controlled the business end of Concord, and Bruce's share of the proceeds was still just trickling in.

Originally, the first three movies had been made for the Southeast Asian and other limited foreign markets. The success of *Enter the Dragon* opened the door in the West, and Raymond Chow seized the opportunity to re-release them to a wider audience. But whether the trickle of proceeds would ever grow to a torrent, and when that would ever happen, was uncertain. Further, the prospect of wrangling with Raymond Chow over a prolonged period on his home turf in Hong Kong probably did not seem like an attractive option. Linda eventually settled with Raymond Chow and sold Bruce's interest in Concord, thus forgoing any future share of the profits from his movies, for a fixed sum. At the time, a bird in the hand was worth more than an uncertain number in the bush.

Then there were the tax authorities, which wanted their slice of Bruce. Since he resided in Hong Kong at the time of death, and had sold his California house, the Hong Kong tax authorities had a claim for its death tax. The State of California also had a claim, since he was arguably still domiciled there, notwithstanding the sale of his house. Bruce died without a will, which complicated the legal picture, but Linda wanted to establish domicile in California.[258] All in all, it took Linda seven years and numerous trips back and forth across the Pacific to complete the probate of his estate.[259]

The estate could do little about all the rip-offs and wannabes that sought to capitalize on Bruce's popularity. A whole sub-genre of Hong Kong exploitation films was spawned using look-alikes with names altered to suggest a connection to Bruce, such as Bruce Le, Bruce Li, Bruce Lai, Bruce Thai and others.[260]

One aspect of the settlement with Raymond Chow was control over the scant footage Bruce had filmed for *Game of Death* before he was side-tracked by *Enter the Dragon*. Working backwards, Chow patched together a story line and hired two look-alikes to shoot all the scenes leading up to the fight scenes Bruce had filmed. To explain the discrepancy in the appearances of the main character, the plot included an assassination attempt which required plastic surgery. The movie was a lackluster hodgepodge until the final scenes featuring Bruce. Even so, when it was released in 1978, the film did well all around the world.[261]

There were some legitimate surfers who rode the wave that Bruce created, such as Jackie Chan, a stuntman on the sets of *Fist of Fury* and *Enter the Dragon*, who became a martial arts star in his own right with his own flare for acrobatic action.[262] And it was not just Asian actors who benefited from Bruce's sudden fame. Chuck Norris, who featured as Bruce's nemesis in *Way of the Dragon*, was given a role in Raymond Chow's *Yellow Faced Tiger* in 1975, after which Norris went on to a long Hollywood career. Likewise, Bob Wall found he had many opportunities to capitalize on his link with Bruce and took advantage of them.

Besides dealing with Bruce's estate, Linda had her own life and that of her children to consider. Eventually Linda went back to school and earned a degree in Political Science at the University of California at Long Beach, then obtained her teaching credentials and taught kindergarten for a while.[263]

Raising two children who were so young when their father died (eight in Brandon's case, four in Shannon's), and helping them navigate through the crosscurrents in his wake, must have been difficult at times. Although Linda tried to downplay their status as children of a world icon, Brandon showed distinct strains of his father's personality and talent, while blazing his own path. Tragically, his promising career was cut short in a gruesome accident while filming his own film, *The Crow*. A gun on the set that was supposed to contain blanks also turned out to have a slug lodged in the barrel. When the gun was pointed at Brandon and fired while shooting a scene, the discharge of the blank propelled the loose slug into his chest. He was only twenty-eight, four years younger than his father was when he passed away. For Linda, such a cruel twist of fate must have been unfathomable.

Shannon went to Tulane and graduated with a degree in music. After pursuing her own career as a singer and actor for a while, she stepped up and took over the reins of managing her father's legacy. It is clear when talking to her that her driving motivation is to preserve his cultural legacy and image, not only as a martial artist but more importantly his message for people to pursue their own dreams.

IN THE MARTIAL arts world, Bruce has of course left a major legacy. Around the world he has fanned an interest in Wing Chun, as the foundational element in his martial arts development. His childhood friend Hawkins Cheung and others have carried on that tradition. The strands of Bruce's Jeet Kune Do, however, are more elusive.

Although he intended to write another book on his martial arts philosophy, and no doubt would have gotten around to it if he had lived longer, he unfortunately never did. *The Tao of Jeet Kune Do*, put together after his death, is a compendium of his writings and thoughts.[264] As such, it gives valuable insight into his approach and how to achieve what he was able to do. But it is not a completed work. That in itself is not a failing—indeed, Bruce would have rejected the notion of any discipline as something that could be completed. Rather, the value of a discipline lay in its capacity to continue to grow.

The only way any discipline can grow is through its practitioners. Although a book can assist, even inspire, a living teacher is immeasurably better, perhaps even essential. The difficulty in finding and training good teachers is one reason Bruce gave up his idea of developing a chain of *gung fu* schools. He realized the importance of the teacher in maintaining the quality of instruction he insisted on. For that reason, he also enjoined the assistant instructors of his three schools not to teach on a commercial basis.

In the years after his death, Taky continued to run the Seattle school in a low-key manner. He ran it initially in the basement of his store on First Hill, with no signage or advertising, as a private club with admission strictly through word of mouth and personal introduction. When he sold his store and moved to Woodinville, he continued to run his classes there.

James Lee, in Oakland, ran his school for a while the same way, but James predeceased Bruce. In Los Angeles, Dan Inosanto also for a long time after Bruce's death ran his school in the manner Bruce approved.

There were other students of Bruce, such as Jesse Glover, who went on to open their own schools. To a greater or lesser degree, each student of Bruce's who continued to teach after his death tried to teach Bruce's approach, while combining it with insights and talents of their own. None of them channeled Bruce, nor would Bruce have wanted them to. Each was his own person, with his own unique skills. But when the torch is passed by them to the next generation, the link to Bruce and his style becomes even more attenuated.

When teaching an approach like Jeet Kune Do, as opposed to a style like Wing Chun or any other distinct system, such an attenuation is no doubt inevitable. It can be viewed as a weakness, but it is also a strength. A strength that forces one to find the right teacher, whatever the particular discipline might be, and to dig into oneself to realize one's own potential. I think Bruce would agree.

But his martial arts legacy cannot be measured by the few schools which can trace their lineage directly to Bruce. Through his films, and the approach to the martial arts they embody, he has both popularized the martial arts as a whole and revolutionized the way it is practiced by many.

The truth is, few could do what Bruce could do even if they learned the techniques that worked for him. Without developing his speed and reflexes, the techniques would not produce the same results. As an example, Bruce was able to move beyond *chi sao* because he had the speed to close the gap and strike without telegraphing, and thus without making contact. Without the same abilities, each person must find his own strengths, and build on them.

One true measure of his legacy is the degree to which martial arts practitioners are still drawing inspiration from him today, nearly 50 years after his death.

———————

PART OF BRUCE'S appeal is that he punched above his weight. He literally punched above his weight, as a welterweight who could physically dominate heavyweights. He also punched above his weight in the movie business.

The standard metric used in the movie business for films is gross revenues, which are hard to pin down for *Enter the Dragon*. Online data bases which compile movie data either don't include the film at all or else contain incomplete numbers.[265] One source puts gross revenues for *Enter the Dragon* at $90 million for 1973, and an estimated $350 million worldwide to date.[266]

But gross revenues are not very meaningful in two respects. In the first place, gross revenues are not adjusted for inflation. This suits the movie industry, since the figures are easy to compare, and allow studios to hype their current movies as "breaking box office records" using inflated dollars.

In the second place, even adjusted revenues do not necessarily provide a meaningful metric, since they say nothing about a film's profitability. One way to measure the profitability of a film is to look at its return on investment, or ROI, which compares its net revenues to its production cost as a percentage. Using this metric, *Enter the Dragon* appears to be one of the top-performing movies of all time.

A recent ranking of films by ROI compiled by *The Numbers* lists *Facing the Giants* as No. 1, with an ROI of 38,451%, down to *Grease* at No. 10 with an ROI of 3,024%.[267] *Enter the Dragon* was apparently not included in the data base used by *The Numbers*, or at least its international earnings were not, perhaps because *The Numbers* did not have access to Concord's sales figures. But if *Enter the Dragon* really generated $350 million world-wide in unadjusted gross revenues, based on its meager production cost of $850,000, its ROI could be as high as 18,429%, which would put it at No. 3 of the top-performing movies of all time.[268] If the weight of a movie is measured by its ROI, *Enter the Dragon* has clearly punched well above its weight.

Bruce probably didn't set his goals in such terms, however. He was prone to frame his goals in a more personal way. In particular, one goal was for *Enter the Dragon* to surpass the movie that Steve McQueen was then working on.[269] In fact, two movies of McQueen's were released around the same time, one at the end of 1972 (*The Getaway*) and one at the end of 1973 (*Papillon*).[270] *Enter the Dragon* out-performed them both in box office sales, and even more spectacularly in terms of ROI, given their higher production costs.[271]

To complete the numbers game, one might look at the rankings of revenues generated by deceased celebrities. Forbes produces such a list every year, which supposedly includes revenues from all sources, including product endorsements as well as album sales, royalties and one-time transactions such as a sale of an estate. The ranking lists the top producers for the year, rather than a cumulative all-time ranking, but is interesting because it gives a glimpse of the enduring nature of some celebrities in the public mind.[272]

Bruce broke into the top ten of the Forbes list in 2013, just behind Steve McQueen, and tied Steve McQueen in 2014 at nine million dollars each. Bruce has not made the Forbes top 13 since then, but has just missed the cut each year, including 2018. McQueen made the list twice more, in 2015 and 2016, and also just missed the cut in 2017, but apparently in 2018 fell below just missing the cut. Again, given Bruce's short time on earth, and only four movies (compared with McQueen's twenty-nine or so), with Shannon's help he appears to be punching well above his weight.

But undoubtedly more important to Bruce than his commercial success was how his movies would be perceived artistically. On that score, he would have been very happy. Upon the release of *Enter the Dragon*, one critic noted Bruce's "charismatic presence." After commenting favorably on some of the other performances, the review goes on to say that it was "Bruce Lee's movie," with his fight sequences "lift[ing] the movie the way Fred Astaire and Rogers used to when they danced in movies of a different fantasy genre."[273]

More recently, another reviewer wrote, "Of course the real showcase here is the obvious star here, Bruce Lee, . . . While Kelly was a famous martial artist and a surprisingly good actor and Saxon was a famous actor and a surprisingly good martial artist, Lee proves to be a master of both fields."[274]

The film's critical acclaim has not diminished over the years. The Best Movies of 1973, as recently compiled by the online *Films 101*, ranks *Enter the Dragon* as No. 14 for films released that year,[275] ahead of McQueen's *Papillon* at No. 30 and Clint Eastwood's *High Plains Drifter* at No. 41. And in *Films 101's* The Best Films of All Time, *Enter the Dragon* ranks No. 688 out of a total of 10,972 films considered (again, ahead of *Papillon* and *High Plains Drifter*).[276] A different ranking, *Empire Magazine's* 2008 list of The 500 Greatest Movies of All Time, ranks *Enter the Dragon* at No. 474.[277]

Perhaps more surprisingly, *Way of the Dragon* also fares well as an enduring critical success, placing No. 24 among *Films 101's* The Best Movies of 1972, and No. 1,571 out of The Best Films of All Time.[278]

Yet another film ranking by *Empire Magazine*, The 100 Best Films of World Cinema, listing the best films not in the English language, ranked *Way of the Dragon* at No. 95, calling it "[a]rguably [Bruce's] greatest film," with "individual set pieces that dominate the film (notably the Chuck Norris gladiatorial fight at the end) [which] are so well choreographed and so well delivered, that nothing else matters much." The list places *Way of the Dragon* in elite company—it includes such all-time classics as Akira Kurosawa's *Seven Samurai*, Ingmar Bergman's *The Seventh Seal*, Federico Fellini's *La Dolce Vita* and Roman Polanski's *Knife in the Water*.

In their own genre, Bruce's films consistently rank among the top. In one 2013 selection *Enter the Dragon* headed the list of ten best martial arts films of all time, ahead of classics like *Yojimbo*, *The Matrix* and *Crouching Tiger, Hidden Dragon*.[279] In another list put together in 2017, it came in second out of fifteen best martial arts movies, just behind *Seven Samurai*. *Fist of Fury* made the same list, at No. 5.[280] Bruce's other movies also often make lists of the all-time best martial arts films.[281]

Since 1973, *Enter the Dragon* has been re-released a number of times in the U.S. and various countries around the world. To this day, it continues to draw viewers.[282]

⸻

SINCE BRUCE DIED so young, before he became a world-wide phenomenon, it is perhaps inevitable to speculate on what he would have done and would be doing now if he were still with us. Surely he would have finished *Game of Death*, and likely turned it into a masterful film that would have surpassed *Enter the Dragon* at the box office. No doubt he would also eventually have expanded his acting and directorial repertoire to themes beyond the martial arts. Bruce himself gave no more than three more years for the *gung fu* craze.[283]

Whether he would have taken up other sports remains an open question. He was not apt to take up any sport unless he thought he could excel.[284] He dabbled with skiing briefly when he flew to Switzerland in 1970 to give private lessons to Roman Polanski, but that was not a sport to which inhabitants of Los Angeles or Hong Kong were easily exposed. When I asked Linda if she thought Bruce would ever have taken up golf, she laughingly dismissed the idea as an endeavor that would have been too slowly paced for him.

He would have almost certainly gotten around to writing a more complete work that expressed his philosophy of the martial arts. His notes, published as *The Tao of Jeet Kune Do*, became widely popular, going through numerous printings.[285] A meticulously completed book would likely have become a masterpiece, perhaps on a level with Musashi's *The Book of Five Rings* that he studied.

Given decades more of life, there would be literally no limit to what he might have accomplished. But the reality is, we only have what he has left us after his brief stay here, which is a lot.

Not only did he single-handedly change the perception of the Asian male in Hollywood and the Western world, in doing so he launched a new genre of action movies in the West and transformed the genre in the East. So totally and rapidly did he captivate the world's imagination, it is easy to forget the brevity of his actual film legacy, with his fourth and last film carrying him to the heights of his post-mortem fame in the West.

But in the end, his greatest accomplishment was personal, both for himself and for the rest of us.

Perhaps we are all diamonds in the rough, or at least raw carbon. Some of us remain un- or only partly polished for our entire lives. A few are shattered during the process of being cut. Bruce's greatest accomplishment was that he applied tremendous pressures to himself that transmuted the raw carbon of his existence into a hardened diamond, and that he then largely cut and polished that diamond himself to become a spectacular gem.

In doing so, he left us his greatest legacy, showing us all what could be done with unassuming raw material through the application of hard work and will power. He showed us a way, his Way, but in doing so gave us each his true message. That we each have our own Way, that we must find for ourselves. He pointed us all at the moon. He walked with some of us part of the way there, and gave us each a push in its direction. Now the rest of the journey is ours to make.

ENDNOTES

257 Jesse too believed Bruce searched for answers after he left Hong Kong that he might not have looked for had he stayed. Bax, *Number One*, p. 83. Linda did too. Linda Lee, *The Bruce Lee Story*, p. 167.

258 If Bruce's estate passed under Hong Kong law, the children would have received a portion of the estate when they turned 21. Linda was not keen on that. Mainly for that reason, Linda took the position that Bruce was still domiciled in California—meaning, that although he had sold his California house and was residing in Hong Kong at the time of his death, he always intended to return to California to live. That became important later when his heirs sought to enjoin rip-off artists who were using Bruce's image to sell various products without permission. A California statute (Section 3344.1 of the California Civil Code) gives strong protection to its citizens' rights of publicity—the right to profit from their own name and likeness.

259 Linda Lee, *The Bruce Lee Story*, p. 188.

260 Polly, *A Life*, p. 481.

261 Ibid., pp. 481-482.

262 His initial movies for Lo Wei, who groomed him to be a successor to Bruce soon after Bruce's death, were unsuccessful. It took him two decades more, with a revamped persona to highlight his comedic talents, before he broke through with *Rumble in the Bronx* to garner a following in the States. Gary Morris (April 1996), "Jackie Chan: *Rumble in the Bronx*," *Bright Lights Film Review*.

263 Linda Lee, *The Bruce Lee Story*, pp. 188-189.

264 A large portion of the book was written by Bruce when he was laid up with his back injury for several months, in 1970. Linda Lee, *The Bruce Lee Story*, p. 169.

265 *BoxOffice Mojo* does not include *Enter the Dragon* in its data base. *The Numbers* cites domestic gross revenues for the film, in the amount of $21,483,063, but does not include any overseas revenues or video sales. *The Numbers'* domestic figures also apparently do not include revenues from re-releases of the movie after 1973.

266 Polly, *A Life*, p. 478. But Polly's source for these figures is not clear. Wikipedia (as accessed on November 24, 2018) gives the same figures ($90 million worldwide for 1973, including $65 million overseas), citing a *Rotten Tomatoes* article, which seems to exclude revenues from Hong Kong. Jen Yamato, "Bruce Lee's *Enter the Dragon* to be Remade," *Rotten Tomatoes*, August 10, 2007. I can find no other source for the $350 million cumulative worldwide estimate.

267 This result was based on estimated net profits for *Facing the Giants* and *Grease* of $38,551,255 and $187,410,137, respectively, and respective production costs of $100,000 and $6,000,000. *Beauty and the Beast* ranked No. 20, with an ROI of 1,974%. *The Numbers*, as accessed November 24, 2018.

268 Reliable net profit figures in the movie industry are notoriously hard to come by. The estimated net profit figures used by *The Numbers* suggests that net profits average around 45% of world-wide revenues, including box office and domestic video sales, at least for films with significant international sales. Applying that profit percentage to *Enter the Dragon's* estimated world-wide revenues of $350 million suggests an ROI of 18,429%. Applying the same methodology to *Avatar* (the highest-grossing film, according to *The Numbers*, as accessed November 24, 2018, with worldwide box office revenues to date of $2.776 billion) to estimate its net profit, including its video sales, and dividing by its production cost of $425 million, its ROI would be a modest 236%.

269 Polly, *A Life*, p. 478.

270 The film score for *The Getaway* was written by Quincy Jones, an alum of Garfield High School, where Linda first saw Bruce.

271 *Enter the Dragon* outgrossed *The Getaway*. Polly, *A Life*, p. 478. Per IMDb, *The Getaway* outgrossed *Papillon*. The production costs for *The Getaway* and *Papillon* were approximately $3,350,000 and $12,000,000, respectively.

272 The revenue numbers cited by Forbes are open to question. The point, however, is not how much money has been generated by Bruce post-mortem. Even if the estimates are inaccurate, they are still indication of his lasting legacy.

273 Alan R. Howard, Review in *The Hollywood Reporter*, August 13, 1973.

274 J.C. Maçek III, "Tournament of Death, Tour de Force: 'Enter the Dragon: 40th Anniversary Edition Blu-Ray,'" *PopMatters*, June 20, 2013.

275 Behind such films as *American Graffiti*, *The Exorcist*, *The Sting* and *Serpico*.

276 Accessed November 29, 2018.

277 I don't think *The Getaway* or *Papillon* made the list, but *The Crow*, starring Bruce's son Brandon, ranked just ahead of *Enter the Dragon*, at No. 468. Bruce would have been proud.

278 Behind *The Godfather*, *Deliverance* and *Last Tango in Paris*, but ahead of McQueen's *Junior Bonner* and *The Getaway*, at No. 40 and No. 63, respectively.

279 "Top 10 Martial Arts Movies," *The Guardian*, December 6, 2013. Accessed November 10, 2018.

280 Aditya Mandhane, "15 Best Martial Arts Movies of All Time," *The Cinemaholic*, August 3, 2017. Accessed November 24, 2018.

281 To cite a couple of other lists that appear in an internet search for the best martial arts films of all time: *Enter the Dragon* at No. 3, *Fist of Fury* at No. 31, *The Big Boss* at No. 43 and *Way of the Dragon* at No. 47, Jim Vorel and Dom Sinacola, "The 100 Best Martial Arts Movies of All Time," *Paste Magazine*, January 29, 2015; and *Enter the Dragon* at No. 4 and *Fist of Fury* (aka *The Chinese Connection*) at No. 6, Abayomi Jegede, "Top 10 Martial Arts Movies of All Time," *Entertainment*, September 18, 2018. There are also some more dubious lists, such as one which includes *The Big Boss* at No. 3 and *Fist of Fury* at No. 5, but does not include *Enter the Dragon* or *Way of the Dragon*. Panos Kotzathanasis, "The 25 Best Martial Arts Movies of All Time," *Taste of Cinema*, May 21, 2016. Not everyone's taste is the same, but the point is, virtually any list of the best martial arts films includes one or more of Bruce's films. And on the lists where his films are edged out of win, place and show, it is usually by different films each time—e.g., by *Seven Samurai* on one list (*The Cinemaholic*), by *Five Deadly Venoms* and *The 36th Chamber of Shaolin* on another (*Paste Magazine*), and by *The 36th Chamber of Shaolin*, *Crouching Tiger, Hidden Dragon* and *Drunken Monkey* II on a third (*Entertainment*).

282 According to the on-line site *IMDb*, the film was re-released in the U.S. in 1979 and 1997, and in other countries around the world at various times. And the film continues to be shown in theaters. As I was finishing this chapter, in November of 2018, a local movie theater in Seattle featured the film several times over the long Thanksgiving weekend.

283 Linda Lee, *The Bruce Lee Story*, p. 155.

284 When Jackie Chan worked as a stuntman on *Fist of Fury*, Bruce apparently ran into him on the street when Jackie was on his way to go bowling. Bruce invited himself along, but after watching Jackie bowl strike after strike, he decided he needed to be somewhere else and left without bowling. Polly, *A Life*, p. 346.

285 Linda Lee, *The Bruce Lee Story*, p. 177.

Acknowledgements

WITHOUT BRUCE AND his friendship, there would obviously be no story. In addition, I will always be in debt for the generosity of his family—especially his father Lee Hoi Chuen, mother Grace, sister Phoebe and brother Robert, who welcomed me with open arms and put up with me for a whole summer in Hong Kong.

Fellow students from the early years are also part of the story. I am grateful to Taky Kimura, a friend from the early Seattle days, who welcomed me back into his class when I returned to Seattle after Bruce's death. I would also like to acknowledge Jesse Glover, Bruce's first student, a humble guy who in his own way epitomized Bruce's message to take what is useful and be true to yourself; and LeRoy Garcia, a good friend of Jesse and also one of the earliest students, who shared some useful insights and is still going strong.

Many others have also helped fill out the account. Linda Lee Cadwell was kind enough to meet and take many hours to patiently answer my questions and then respond to numerous follow-up emails. Daughter Shannon Lee and her team at the Bruce Lee Foundation—Sydnie Wilson and Jess Scott and Kris Storti—bent over backwards to allow me access to Bruce's daytimers and other records and photos, some of which appear in this book.

Over the years David Tadman has also provided me photos I didn't have, some of which are in this book.

My brother Mike and high-school friend Lanston Chinn helped fill in some perspective on Bruce from his Seattle days. Jacquie Kay, Lanston's cousin, who introduced me to Bruce, helped refresh my memory on some early details.

Perry Lee, an unparalleled collector of Bruce Lee memorabilia, with whom I trained decades ago at Taky's Seattle school, has been unstinting in providing relevant books and articles that I would never have otherwise uncovered.

My daughter Kari and son-in-law Rob Weinsheimer, both medical doctors, have been very supportive of the project and extremely helpful in parsing through the medical information and speculation surrounding Bruce's death and prior collapse.

Ryosuke Komori provided a platform with his Digiletter website to begin writing about my time with Bruce. And Bruce Rutledge of Chin Music Press provided sage advice in how to revise the digiletters into a book format.

Finally, I would be remiss not to profoundly thank my wife Noriko. Without her persistence and gentle prodding over the years, this book may never have come to be.

DOUG PALMER GREW up in Seattle, where he met and learned *gung fu* from Bruce Lee. While attending Yale University, he spent a summer with Bruce and his family in Hong Kong. After graduating with a major in Chinese Studies and obtaining a law degree from Harvard Law School, he worked in Tokyo for 4½ years. He returned to practice law in Seattle for the next few decades, and is now enjoying his retirement.